D1536659

A Culinary History of
PITTSBURG COUNTY

LITTLE ITALY, CHOCTAW BEER
and LAMB FRIES

DAVID CATHEY

AMERICAN PALATE

Published by American Palate
A Division of The History Press
Charleston, SC 29403
www.historypress.net

Unless otherwise noted, images appear courtesy of the author.

First published 2013

Manufactured in the United States

ISBN 978.1.62619.162.4

Library of Congress CIP data applied for.

For my little quarter bambinos, Luke and Kate; Lori, my love; and to my mother, Lila, who always knew I had it in me.

CONTENTS

ACKNOWLEDGEMENTS

This project was made possible by Becky LeJeune at The History Press, to my great fortune. Her guidance and extreme patience has been integral to its completion. My wife, Lori, has talked me off the ledge more than once and, like me, has come to hold the town of Krebs in a special place in the heart that we share.

Because this book was written long after the death of its principal players, works in *Oklahoma Today* magazine, *Chronicles of Oklahoma* and by colleagues past and present at the *Oklahoman* were heavily leaned on to capture the voice of the dearly departed.

Kenny Brown's *The Italians in Oklahoma* was crucial to developing an understanding of not only the coal industry and its pull on the Italians but also the culture of those times. Because this book was completed under a very tight schedule, Steven Sewell's article "Choctaw Beer: Tonic or Devil's Brew?" from the *Journal of Cultural Geography*, was invaluable—not to mention highly entertaining. It's worth finding for further reading on the rollicking period from which the legend of Choc beer sprang.

My good friend Julie Wheeler, a brilliant journalist in hiding, encapsulated the book in one sentence. Well played, Judge Julie, and thanks. Thanks to "The Dale," a true Ironhead from just north of Pittsburg County. Your contribution was, of course, noted.

A special thanks to the Pittsburg County Historical Society and the families who shared their stories, including the DeFranges, Fassinos, Finamores, Giacomos, Lallis, Loveras, Peccios and Prichards. Their legacies are the foundation of this book and, very likely, the town of Krebs, Oklahoma. The coal belt that runs from Missouri to north Texas is dotted with ghost towns. McAlester might've swallowed up Krebs years ago without the resolve of those families and the others who still make up the community that bears the heart of Pittsburg County's culinary history.

INTRODUCTION

The Indian Nation Turnpike crosses U.S. Highway 69 between the McAlester Army Munitions Post and the southwestern edge of McAlester, the county seat of Pittsburg County in southeastern Oklahoma, where every May a huge Italian festival is held. This X marks the spot where a fledgling former coal-mining boomtown was saved by a federal installation that produces practically every bomb in the U.S. Army arsenal, supplying a second major employer in a community that desperately needed it when it was established in 1943. The other major employer is just a few miles back north on the turnpike and east on U.S. Highway 270. As you travel east on this lonesome strip of highway that cuts through the green hills, you pass a monument to the prison rodeo held at Big Mac, otherwise known as the Oklahoma State Penitentiary, that's just ahead and to the north. The rodeo is held behind the walls of the prison, covered by ESPN when its programming included professional billiards, lumberjack competitions and Australian Rules football. The menacing white installation at the foot of a rise on the prairie is spangled in razor wire—the very prison fictional Tom Joad is released from in the early portion of John Steinbeck's *The Grapes of Wrath*. A 1973 prison riot at Big Mac lasted for three days and is mentioned among the worst in American history. It makes for a striking—if not hospitable—entryway to the heart of Pittsburg County. A little farther down that highway, you pass the Pittsburg County Courthouse and a string of law offices that has to be seen to be believed for a town whose population doesn't crack twenty thousand.

A munitions outpost, more than one-hundred-year-old penitentiary and lawyers' nest doesn't scream culinary lynchpin. But relief is just a few more miles away.

According to George Nigh, a former multi-term governor of Oklahoma who was born and raised in McAlester, Pittsburg County was named by a train conductor making a stop in the days before the town or county had a proper name but plenty of bituminous coal.

"This conductor supposedly looked out at the area and said, 'This place looks just like Pittsburgh [Pennsylvania],'" Nigh says. "We like to say we knocked the 'h' out of Pittsburgh."

McAlester gets its name from J.J. McAlester, who later became lieutenant governor of Oklahoma and was immortalized as a character in the Charles Portis novel *True Grit* and the subsequent Oscar-nominated films made in 1969 and 2010.

But the culinary heart of Pittsburg County isn't related to Western novels, bomb plants or hoosegows. And it's not rooted in McAlester.

That honor resides a little farther on U.S. 270, across an overpass on the eastern edge of McAlester in neighboring Krebs, home of the Terrapin Derby, originated in 1929 when Mayor J.T. Sadler visited the Miller Brothers Shows in Ponca City and brought the derby back to Krebs as a fundraising idea for the fire department. Krebs also had an Italian band that played in a double-decker bandstand in downtown Krebs. There were at least five bandstands between McAlester and Hartshorne that the band frequented on weekends. Krebs also featured prominently in Elmore Leonard's 2005 gangster novel *The Hot Kid*. But Krebs' biggest claim to fame is its food culture, which sprouted from the seed of hardship into a fully bloomed cuisine that thrives today. Hardship and tragedy came from the coal that first drew entrepreneurs, then railroads and finally immigrant workers. While the coal boom lasted long enough to draw several thousand native Italians, it couldn't navigate the Scylla and Charybdis that was the rise of oil and the Great Depression. But the Italians did.

Compared to the day-to-day hardships and tragedies these immigrants faced and conquered, finding new work and living in extreme frugality was nothing. Besides, the southern Italians had been surviving in similar hopeless environs for hundreds of years back home. They applied the same survival tactics used there, sticking to what they knew. And what they knew best was food.

Before Nigh was elected governor, he spent several terms as lieutenant governor. He recalled hosting the National Lieutenant Governors Conference in Pittsburg County.

"I rented out all the restaurants in Krebs," he recalled. "We filled up every one of the restaurants with dignitaries from all over the country. I remember my wife, Donna, and I walking from one restaurant to the other, because they're all so close together you could do that, and welcoming everyone to the food capital of Oklahoma.

"Everyone loved it," Nigh said. "It truly was a highlight of my career in hosting people in Oklahoma and showing off Pittsburg County."

This book aims to pick up where Governor Nigh left off, sharing the story of how a handful of families cultivated a thriving culinary tradition in Pittsburg County by watering seeds of hardship with sweat equity to maintain their community. Whether you stop for a steak at GiaComo's, a Choc at Pete's Place, lamb fries at the Isle of Capri, gnocchi at Roseanna's or a coil of sausage and a gourd of caciocavallo at Lovera's, it will be in a venue impervious to the effects of time. The magic of the food culture of Pittsburg County isn't in its pushing forth of cuisine but rather holding fast and carrying on in a fast-changing world. The past is alive, well and delicious in Pittsburg County.

Chapter 1

FRONTIER SURVIVAL

A light snow fell over Krebs, Oklahoma, in late October 1930. Otherwise, Marta Lovera wouldn't have had any notion where to find the hog missing from her yard. The pig's tracks trailed through the snow, but so, too, did the tracks of those she feared had stolen it. It was unthinkable to leave a commodity as valuable as a hog unattended in such depressed economic times. Marta and her husband, Battista, had left northern Italy twenty-three years previous with little more than entrepreneurial spirit and the names of a few friends and family who had preceded them to America. In that time, they'd celebrated enough success and suffered enough failure to have their priorities in order. And a hog was undoubtedly a commodity of incredible value.

The early snow would've signaled the end of this hog's life and the beginning of the Lovera family's winter preparations. Marta would do as she'd been taught growing up in northern Italy. First, she would butcher the hog and grind it with fresh garlic and ground black pepper to make sausage. The casings came from the hog's intestines. The lard would be rendered down in a large crock. The sausages would be submerged in the lard and moved into a cellar. There the lard would set and offer preservation for the sausages all winter. Born in Italy, the method worked just as efficiently on the southeastern Oklahoma frontier.

But frontiers are always fraught with peril, and the coal belt that stretched from Missouri to Texas, cutting a swath through the verdant hills of the Choctaw Nation, was no different. Darwin's theory was proven every day in the rugged hill country, which Marta and the two small children she led

through the snow had learned firsthand just days before when a blast in the Wheatley Sample No. 4 Coal Mine in nearby McAlester took the lives of thirty men, including her husband, Battista, and their oldest son, Simone, who everyone called Sam. As devastating as that ordeal had been, coming home from burying her breadwinners to find missing the hog that would sustain Marta; her twelve-year-old daughter, Mary; and ten-year-old son, Matteo was an immediate indication of just how difficult surviving the frontier would be.

Four years later, Rose Giacomo would come to the same stark realization when her husband, Jim, died, leaving her to raise six children. The only good news for either Marta or Rose was that they had seen how widows survived after the mines took the lives of their loved ones: they cooked. Some had multiple specialties, while others concentrated on a few:

Top: Marta Lovera. *Courtesy of the Lovera family.*

Bottom, from left: Mike, Marta and Mary Lovera, who survived in Oklahoma's coal country thanks to Marta's sausage recipe and Choctaw beer. *Courtesy of the Lovera family.*

sausage, cheese and bread were the staple dishes they'd learned to make in the Old Country and brought with them to Indian Territory. But the newly arrived immigrants wouldn't find sufficient conditions to grow grapes for table wine. In Oklahoma's coal country, a different libation was on the lips of practically every hard-working coal miner, Choctaw beer.

"Everyone made Choc beer," said Dominica Lovera, whose grandfather Carmine Finamore was a prominent butcher and livestock rancher in what would eventually become Pittsburg County. "Everyone had their own recipe. You'd have to go around and taste everybody's. They'd have some cheese or sausage or bread, too. We'd go around and try everybody's and decide whose was best."

Who made it the best? Ask around town, and the name that pops up the most is Ruthie Fabrizio.

"Hers was the best," said Karen Scarpitti, who grew up in and around her grandmother Minnie Peccio's restaurant, Minnie's Italian Dinners.

While the Fabrizio family made the most popular Choc in town, Karen's grandmother and Pete Prichard, who came to Indian Territory as a child named Pietro Piegari, followed suit and eventually established the first two major Krebs restaurants: Minnie's Italian Dinners and Pete's Place.

A mining accident just missed taking Pete Prichard's life but injured him severely enough that he could no longer descend into the mines teeming with bituminous coal. Pete had an advantage in drawing the miners away from other Choc houses, as he'd once been one himself. He knew the guys and knew what they liked to eat and drink. And Pete's larger-than-life personality made him a popular *paisan*. Five years before Marta Lovera lost her husband, and nine years before Rose lost hers, Pete opened a proper restaurant out of his house thanks to the growing success of the Choc he started brewing in 1919 and the foods he started preparing in the interim. The fare was an amalgamation of foods that sustained two different cultures: Old World Italians and New World cattlemen.

Today, four generations of Prichards have upheld the culinary tradition started by their patriarch in two restaurants with more than 120 years of combined service. Four generations have followed Rose Giacomo's heroic stand on the frontier in two other restaurants, serving the cuisine that's come to be synonymous with modern-day Pittsburg County: ravioli, spaghetti, meatballs, lamb fries and Choc beer. Marta Lovera would survive the hardest winter of her life and eventually marry into a small grocery store that little Matteo, who everyone called Mike, would eventually build into a business that thrived forty years and continues to expand under the direction of the son he named after his brother who was buried that fateful October day in 1930.

The coal boom wouldn't last, but Pittsburg County would eventually become home to two major sources of employment: the Oklahoma State Penitentiary and what is now the McAlester Army Ammunition Plant. As luck would have it, three of Oklahoma's most prominent politicians would all rise out of what would come to be known as Little Dixie. The uncanny number of sons of Pittsburg County who grew up to become power brokers played a prominent role in supporting and publicizing the culinary tradition of the area. If it's true that the best way to learn a community's story is through its food, then the story of Oklahoma's Pittsburg County begins in the tiny town of Krebs. Three restaurants in this town of 2,053, according to the 2010 census, plus another in neighboring McAlester (population 18,383) will serve between 3,000 and 5,000 people most weekends. In other rural communities throughout the Deep South and Southwestern United States, dining crowds of that magnitude would likely be lining up for steaks, barbecue or all-you-can-eat catfish.

Once you take the overpass past the George Nigh Expressway, U.S. 270 splits from U.S. 69. A median at the crossroads bears a sign flanked by two old-fashioned streetlights that reads, "Welcome to Oklahoma's Little Italy." Taking Exit 69, the access road winds, dips and rises into Krebs. Where the road rises on the edge of town, there is a small hill topped by an abandoned house flanked by large oak trees. A neon sign that hasn't lit up in decades hangs over the porch that reads, "Minnie's Italian Dinners." While Minnie Peccio's old restaurant hasn't been in operation since the 1970s, the house where the young, single mother sold Old World Italian food, Choc beer and homemade wine for four decades is the first whisper of the rich past that awaits. Minnie's opened about 1930 and closed about 1970, and according to "Mama Peck's" grandson Dominic Silva Jr., it's where the locals ate, drank and danced until dawn.

Just east of the hill Minnie's haunts, you'll quickly come upon an enormous yellow house. This is Pete's Place. Always has been, can't imagine it will ever be anything else. The color remains the same as it was in 1925, but the house has grown ten-fold since the first time Pietro Piegari served a cold glass of Choctaw beer from a backroom. Today, Pete's Place takes up about thirteen thousand square feet in the same spot where Pietro once had a little house in the sticks. The restaurant is made up of about thirty private dining rooms, which accommodate parties large and small. When the rooms fill up, which they routinely do every weekend, Joe and Kathy Prichard open up the large banquet room to accommodate up to about five hundred diners who have come from far and near to eat Old World Italian fare with lamb fries and

Entering the town of Krebs in Pittsburg County, a sign welcomes visitors to Oklahoma's Little Italy.

Minnie's Italian Dinners operated from the early 1930s to the early 1970s.

maybe some steak and fried chicken, along with a hand-crafted beer from the Krebs Brewing Company next door. From outside the brewery, you don't even have to squint to read the bright neon sign lighting up the night just a few hundred feet east: the Isle of Capri.

Pete's Place is the oldest and largest of Pittsburg County's legendary restaurants. *Courtesy of the Prichard family.*

The Isle of Capri opened on Mother's Day 1950 in Krebs.

This is where Dominic Anthony Giacomo paid tribute to his mother back in 1950 with a restaurant that served the same Old World foods using recipes his family brought from Italy in 1895. The Isle of Capri and its unmistakable Frank Lloyd Wright–inspired architecture haven't changed much in the past sixty-plus years, though it is much larger than when it first opened. When you walk through the front door today, you'll be greeted by Rose Ann Robertson, Dom's niece, seated behind a desk just a few steps inside, with a big smile and quick, "Hello, honey." Rose Ann and her family still do things the way Uncle Dom did them. They figure there's no use changing something that's supported a large family for this long.

No human could survive visits to both the Isle of Capri and Pete's Place in a day, but no one who visits Krebs will want to leave without bringing a piece of it home. A block north to Washington, two more two blocks east on Sixth and a few hundred feet north, you'll roll up on an unassuming native stone

Lovera's Italian Market has served Pittsburg County since 1946.

building built in 1910 where Lovera's Italian Market has stood since 1946. A red, white and green awning drapes over the porch outside the first floor of the small two-story 103-year-old building with the Lovera's name stenciled on the window. When the door swings open, time stops, or at least slows nearly to a crawl. Caciocavera gourds tied to each end of yellow ropes drape over piping high above the meat counter. Below the house-made cheese are cold cuts from the Old Country and sausage from the factory out back. The shelves are stocked with Italian specialties, house olive oils and sauces. Years come and go, but the feeling in this market remains rooted in the rich history of Oklahoma's early days in coal country.

On the east end of town, you'll find Roseanna's, opened by one of Pietro Piegari's sons, Frank, and his family of twelve back in 1975. No family has more of its members dedicated day-to-day to serving the frontier fusion set by their patriarch in 1925.

Go back across the 270 bridge and curl around the south exit down to the George Nigh Expressway along the edge of neighboring McAlester and you'll find GiaComo's, which was opened in 1959 by Dom Giacomo and run for years by his brother Nick Giacomo. This was Dom's design and his

Above: Roseanna's is the youngest of Krebs' historic restaurants, opening originally in 1975.

Left: GiaComo's, located in McAlester, opened in 1959.

crowning achievement, next to the futuristic service station he built next door. Dom's niece Dora Lea Brewer and her son Wendell Brewer keep the Rat Pack–friendly atmosphere bustling into the twenty-first century, which might some day live up to the vision of the future Dom foresaw.

Pittsburg County is home to an authentic fusion of Old World–style Italian fare and prairie survival food that took root in the hills of southeastern Oklahoma in the 1870s and is alive and thriving today as well as it ever has been. In the Krebs Heritage Museum, curated by Steve DeFrange, you can peruse the roster of the 1916 Societa' Italiana Di M.S. Cristoforo Colombo Di Krebs, which boasts surnames that could be confused with a menu at a Sicilian pastry shop: Contratto, Fabrizio, Fiori and Sicoletti. The men worked hard, played hard and helped each other survive. Today, the legacy of those stark Darwinian days is told at four restaurants and a grocery store within a five-mile radius that share the stories of their ancestors through homemade sausage, cheese and heaping plates of pasta, meatballs, ravioli, sausage, steak, fried chicken and lamb fries.

While Italian food was what they knew how to cook, lamb fries were what they learned to love. If you're thinking lambs don't have fries, you're obviously correct. Lamb fries are a gentle term for thin-sliced lamb testicles

The food in Pittsburg County illustrates the collision of classic frontier foods from the west and Old World southern Italy.

Pete's Place is home to the Krebs Brewing Company. *Courtesy of the Prichard family.*

that are battered, deep-fried and served with fresh lemon wedges. It's not Old World Italian, but it's definitely old-school frontier food. The Italians weren't the only ones who'd learned to sustain themselves on meager rations. Oklahoma was and is in the heart of livestock country. Cattle's primal cuts were a precious commodity to ranchers, so learning to appreciate these less-attractive assets was a necessity.

And just when you think you've got a bead on Oklahoma's Little Italy, it throws you a bender. What's that they're drinking in Krebs? Local wine? Not quite. This Italian community didn't stomp grapes: it brewed Choctaw beer, whose murky origin help enrich Krebs mythology.

Today, Pittsburg County is diversified by the large Italian population that was at its greatest between 1870 and 1930. The Choctaw Nation affords the county the opportunity to have a casino, and nearby lakes keep it within striking distance of weekend tourists and travelers. The county's lush, verdant prairie lands offer rich natural resources and attract rural sensibilities.

While old-timers might say Pittsburg County ain't what it used to be, that might not be a bad thing. Time has cleared it of the misery of coal mining and left behind the best part of the past, including a culinary tradition from a bygone era. This is the story of the families who carry on that tradition one plate of pasta with a side of lamb fries and a cold Choc beer at a time.

Chapter 2

OLD WORLD ITALIAN FOOD ON THE NEW WESTERN FRONTIER

Italian cuisine is ancient, predating the birth of the United States by centuries. There is a certain American arrogance that takes for granted civilization formed before a boatload of angry Pilgrims bumped into a rock anchored along the coast of what is now Plymouth, Massachusetts. In fact, the view of Italian food among Americans has wavered drastically since Thomas Jefferson and friends first slurped a strand of spaghetti. A myriad of scholarly papers have been written on the assimilation or lack thereof of Italian cuisine to American palates, and this book doesn't intend to examine the phenomena in full. But too often, restaurants like Pete's Place, the Isle of Capri, Roseanna's and GiaComo's in Pittsburg County are wrongly dismissed as Americanized Italian. Joe Prichard, whose grandfather was the founder of Pete's Place, points out that his father came to the United States in 1903, and the food he served to make a living was a combination of foods available in a rural setting and the foods his family had been preparing for generations in southern Italy. And those foods are ravioli, tomato sauce, meatballs, homemade sausage, spaghetti and homemade cheese.

These days, Old World southern Italian food is often mistakenly dismissed, the same way Tex-Mex cuisine is, because it has been present in this country for so long that it *must've* been bastardized. Prichard is quick to point out that you'll never find a meatball served in a bed of pasta and under a thick blanket of tomato sauce anywhere in Italy, and pasta tends to be overcooked in this country, but the dishes his family and those at the Isle of Capri, Roseanna's and GiaComo's make today are the same dishes his grandfather, who was born in southern Italy, made back in 1925. So, the question remains: why is southern Italian food so much more historically pervasive in this country than northern Italian food, which has only come to the attention of the American palate in the last half of the twentieth century?

In a word: politics.

Italy was in the midst of tremendous political upheaval when its residents from the south began a mass exodus across the Atlantic Ocean to Ellis Island in the late nineteenth century. Italy was in the process of unifying, and the south regions were poorer and more rural than those to the north. Folks from the regions of Abruzzi, Basilicata, Calabria, Campania and Sicily felt that the north held an economic advantage that made staying in Italy impossible. So the southern Italians went west, looking for opportunity in the New World. And they brought with them the foods and practices that had sustained them through a life of hardship.

These practices included gardening, which led to cooking by the seasons; curing and canning, which stretched the shelf life of precious resources; and creating dishes that stretched ingredients. The foods and the practices were well rehearsed and carried a proven track record of sustaining peasants over hundreds of years. According to Anna Del Conte's 1976 book *Portrait of Pasta*, the first known Italian food writer was a Greek Sicilian named Archestratus from Syracuse in the fourth century BCE. He wrote a poem about "top quality and seasonal" ingredients. For centuries, Romans employed Greek bakers to produce breads, imported cheeses from Sicily, commonly reared goats for butchering and grew artichokes and leeks.

The foods evolved with advances in technology and leaps of creativity, resulting in the aforementioned staples of southern Italy. Unlike other immigrants who preceded them into the United States, the Italians had no intention of giving up their favorite foods. The New World might've offered improved opportunities to earn a living, but from the Italian view, it offered little in the way of food. Italian food was a source of cultural pride, handed down over generations. Not only was it superior to the cuisine popular across the Atlantic, but it also was developed in peasant villages by those who had proven most fit to survive. Peasants developed techniques for gardening, canning, preserving, drying and curing in the Old World out of necessity but found the results as delicious as they were efficient. Whether they become comfort foods thanks to their association with survival or profound deliciousness is impossible to know. The truth is the two factors are likely linked. Regardless, the Italians weren't giving up their culinary traditions, and it was a good thing because while opportunities in the New World outnumbered those back home, the lifestyle was far from lavish. Conditions were particularly grim on frontiers, where those who didn't speak English were able to find work on railroads, in industrial factories and in coal mines.

As popular and celebrated as Italian food is today, it was initially snubbed and criticized by the gatekeepers of the American household preceding the turn of the twentieth century. So, the Little Italys dotting large cities, the industrial strip and coal belt in post–Civil War America were where Italian food stayed for close to half a century. In a chapter of the book *Food in the USA* called "The American Response to Italian Food, 1880–1930," author Harvey Levenstein points out that Italian chefs were well established in fine hotels in large U.S. cities, but their menus didn't reflect their heritage. Levenstein explains that images of rough-and-tumble immigrants who dug ditches and sewers while living crammed in tenements in crime-ridden neighborhoods overseen by the band of "the Black Hand" had devastated the collective unconscious perception of Italy as the land of gondoliers and Renaissance-era palazzos. Levenstein writes, "Spaghetti could stay on the menu, but only as 'Italienne,' the French spelling bringing some reassurance that the original Italian dish had been civilized and purified in French hands." So, it's no surprise the first successful mass producer of canned spaghetti was Franco-American.

For a short time during the 1880s, tomatoes were believed to be carcinogenic,[1] but even after that was disproved, experts warned that tomatoes carried an "oxalic acid" that made them harmful.[2] Levenstein reviewed numerous nineteenth-century issues of Good Housekeeping to unearth gems like this from 1890: "As an article of food, pork, of late years, does not generally meet the approval of intelligent people as is almost entirely discarded by hygienists." Levenstein also points out Italian affection for fresh fruit and green vegetables wasn't embraced in the United States, as nutritionists of the day had not yet discovered the benefits of whole foods, dismissing them as expensive and lacking nutritional value as they were made up almost completely of water.

As the voice of the prohibitionists rose, so, too, did sentiment damning spicy foods as a gateway to alcohol consumption. There was thought that spicy foods might overstimulate and wear out the nervous system. Garlic didn't become the main deterrent to vampires in legend because it tasted good. Despite its popularity today, garlic was once viewed as a malodorous deterrent to good taste, on and off the plate. Even in Italy, the use of spices

1. Harvey Levenstein, "The American Response to Italian Food," in *Food USA*, edited by Carole M. Counihan, 78 (New York: Routledge, 2002).
2. J.M. Albahary, Annales des Falsifications et des fraudes 2, no. 5 (1909): 140–44, abstract in U.S. Department of Agriculture, Office of Experimentations, Record 22 (January–June 1910): 264.

was associated with wealth and importance, leaving garlic and onions to the peasants.[3] In his 2008 book, *Delizia!: The History of Italians and Their Food,* author John Dickie writes, "This is not to imply the well-to-do refused to eat these pungent vegetables—they just looked down on anyone who had no alternative when it came to flavoring food." Mixing foods was thought to make them more difficult to digest, which made one-pot meals a no-no on the nineteenth-century American table. A pamphlet circulated by the New York association in 1914 warned that mixing foods together robbed them of their nutritive effects. "It is not right to cook meat, cheese, beans and macaroni together," it said. It further suggested delicatessens should be avoided altogether because spicy foods like salami, sausage, pickles and potato salads damaged the stomach without providing any sustenance.[4]

Native-born American laborers considered the soups and stews their Italian co-workers commonly consumed as "pig wash," despite the assurance of prominent nutritionist Mary Hinman Abel that these foods were not only delicious but healthful. Cheese, so common in the Italian repertoire, was considered practically indigestible by Americans in the early years of the Italian influx, according to Levenstein. Regardless, the Italians refused to assimilate in culinary matters, and it would take the passing of a generation before the rest of the country finally realized why.

At the outset of World War I, there was a movement to conserve household staples like meats, wheat flour and sugar. Social workers were deployed nationwide, including in the immigrant camps and communities, to lecture and instruct on conservation techniques. The Italian community had little use for these instructions because conservation and efficiency had long ago been established in their predominantly peasant lineage. Levenstein writes, "In September 1917 the Vernacular Press section refused to circulate an article calling for reduced consumption of meat ('We Can Fight Back with Our Teeth') because 'practically all the readers of the foreign language press already ate very little meat because they couldn't afford to eat much of it.'" A similar campaign to promote planting Victory Gardens met with a similar collective eye roll from Italians, as cultivating food from seed was as common as waking up in the morning in Italian households.

By 1918, the Italians had won the argument, though no concession was ever given by the same household gatekeepers who had dismissed their food in

---

3. John Dickie, *The Delizia!: The Epic History of the Italians and Their Food* (New York: Free Press, 2008), 3.
4. Winnifred S. Gibbs, "Dietetics in Italian Tenements," *Public Health Nurse Quarterly* 6, no. 1 (1914).

previous years. Levenstein points out that magazines like *Good Housekeeping* started routinely publishing articles that used Italians as examples of exemplary food conservation. "Meatless days have no terror for our Italian friends" began a *Good Housekeeping* feature on spaghetti and ravioli preparation, which went on to state, "Ravioli, favorite dish of our Italian ally, should be served on every American table."[5] Once criticized for the intensity of flavor and expensive ingredients, Italian cooks were now the model of frugality.

In 1919, author Francis Clark wrote a book called *Our Italian Fellow Citizens* in defense of Italian immigrants. When it came to food, Clark wrote of the Italians, "The [Italian] housewife will make a cabbage and a knuckle go farther than most native Americans would make a loin of beef and a half dozen vegetables…Nothing is too coarse or repulsive for the Italian peasant to eat, if it is not absolutely poison…squid and octopus, though tough and leathery, are not such hideous things to eat as they are to look at." As for cooking polenta, he wrote there were more ways of cooking pasta and polenta than there were ways to cook eggs, "and each way of cooking it seems a little better than the last."

The 1920s also saw advancement in nutritional guidelines. Previous diets recommending heavy intake of proteins were revised to include a balance of fruit, vegetables and dairy, which was right in the wheelhouse of the Italian diet. By the middle of that decade, the view of Italian cuisine was in full reverse, and Italian food was the cuisine du jour. Canned Italian foods from companies like Franco-American became a favorite of small children, laying the foundation for a new generation of Americans who would grow up with a taste for spaghetti and meatballs. Italians refused to give up their culinary traditions, which eventually became revered for their flavor and efficiency. Subsequently, Italian food became the first widely accepted and beloved cuisine from a foreign country. French cuisine was first to find acceptance in the United States but not with the wide-ranging success of Italian, which became a staple meal in American households then and now. If there was bastardization of Italian foods, it was done by the manufacturers, not the turn of the century cooks or restaurateurs.

Since the early days of the Italian immigration, Italian "restaurants" materialized in rooming houses that catered to the palates of those from specific regions of Italy, including in Krebs. Levenstein hypothesized that as regional allegiances among immigrants weakened the longer they stayed in this country, the foods of the predominant immigrants came to the forefront. That would be the southern Italian fare of Campania and Sicily. And it's these foods that the town of Krebs became known for, starting in 1925, and demand for it there has yet to slow.

---

5. Elsinore Crowell, "Peppers and Garlic," *Good Housekeeping* 65 (September 1918): 64, 121.

But that's not the only food you'll find in the iconic restaurants of Pittburg County. Today, the restaurants serve more Italian fare than they did in their earliest days. One day, at lunch with Joe Prichard and Sam Lovera, we sampled the Krebs staples: lamb fries, ravioli, spaghetti and meatballs, antipasto and salad. Sammy took a break and said, "It's just peasant food. Folks couldn't afford anything fancy, but if you cook the same thing over and over for thirty years, you get pretty good at it. That's all it is—and I love it. I eat it all the time."

Those who came to Krebs from Italy came from humble lineage: shepherds, men of trade and storekeepers. They became frontiersmen disguised as coal miners with an entrepreneurial spirit in common and a love of food and drink as part of their DNA. Regardless of which direction their dreams pointed them, the foods they loved were the same. The four restaurants that still operate via the Prichard and Giacomo families all serve the aforementioned dishes from old family recipes, but their ancestors weren't eating steak, fried chicken and lamb fries in southern Italy.

Once upon a time, Oklahoma's immigrants from Italy were accused of refusing to assimilate to their new surroundings because they banded together in trade, maintained Catholicism in a land rife with Protestants, hadn't yet learned the native language and even went to added expense to ensure they ate their own food. Those accusations were proven shortsighted when the Italians of Pittsburg County turned out in droves to enlist at the dawn of World War II and by the ongoing residence of Italians in the area today. The menus at the restaurants in Krebs were also proof of the Italians' intentions to stick around and grow their businesses.

When Pete's Place opened in 1925, it featured Italian specialties, but owner Pete Prichard was quick to add items popular with non-Italians, like steak, chicken and lamb fries. When Dom Giacomo opened the Isle of Capri many years later, he followed Pete's lead and even added hand-cut, oven-roasted French fries that his niece Rose Ann Robertson says they tried to take off the menu, but people just kept asking for them so they left it alone. Wendell Brewer, who runs GiaComo's with his mother, Dora Lea, said his top two sellers are steak and lamb fries.

Together, these frontier survival foods form the basis for Krebs' cuisine, which likely began with ravioli, which each restaurant makes from a family recipe. While it's impossible to know the first dish Pete Prichard ever served, ravioli would be a safe guess considering it's one of the oldest of southern Italy's delicacies. Although ravioli is the result of a time-tested preparation, it is also indicative of the efficiency of Italian peasant food. It's easy to imagine an ancient Italian matriarch stuffing cost-effective pasta flour with cheese, leftovers or small

Pete's Place was originally in a thicket of trees. *Courtesy of the Prichard family.*

ground portions of secondary cuts to stretch the cupboard's contents with no loss of flavor. Good food makes for happy workers, and since practically all these frugal folks did was work, food was essential to happiness as well as survival. In Ortensio Lando's Catalogo de gli inventori delle cose che si mangiano (Catalog of inventors of things that may be eaten), he attributes the invention of ravioli to a peasant woman from Lombardy, saying, "Libista,[6] a peasant woman from Cernuschio, was the inventor of ravioli wrapped in dough."

In Krebs, ravioli is boiled, toasted or fried, and it's always served with tomato sauce. Pasta has been synonymous with tomato sauce in the United States since Franco-American canned its first mishmash of the two. But tomato sauce is less authentic to Italy than most things on the menu of any Italian restaurant. The tomato was brought to Europe by the Spanish upon their initial conquests of the New World. It was quickly adopted anywhere it could be grown, and Italy was among its most enthusiastic adopters. Turns out, tomato sauce works great with all kinds of pasta, so the food in Krebs reflects a stage of evolution in Italian cuisine. And just as Belgians eat pommes frites with dipping sauces other than ketchup, so, too, do we eat our pasta and tomato sauce differently than they do in Italy.

---

6. Alberto Capatti and Massimo Montanari, *Italian Cuisine: A Cultural History*, trans. A.N. O'Healy (New York, Columbia University Press, 2003): 63.

Perhaps the first superstar of Italian cuisine in the United States was spaghetti and meatballs. For many in this country, spaghetti is Italian food, thanks to the aforementioned folks at Franco-American and their competitor Chef Boyardee. But there is great disagreement on whether spaghetti and its pasta paisans are authentic to the Mediterranean or strictly the result of the contents of Marco Polo's goodie bag brought back from China. Whether it was ancient Etruscans, who preceded the Italians on the boot-shaped republic on the western edge of the Mediterranean Sea, or the Chinese who are responsible for introducing Italians to pasta, the result is the same: Italians perfected it. Its consumption in Sicily was first referenced in 1154. Unleavened dough or durum wheat flour mixed with water, formed into sheets of various shapes and then cooked in hot water is the method, and it has proven to be one of the world's most popular foods. The popularity of pasta spread to the rest of Italy after the establishment of pasta factories in the nineteenth century, enabling the mass production of pasta for the Italian market.[7]

One thing they do in Krebs that is consistent with the rest of the era in which Italian food first came to prominence but is unheard of in Italy is to combine meatballs with pasta and tomato sauce. In Italy, meatballs are generally eaten as a main course or in a soup. The main ingredients of an Italian meatball are typically beef and/or pork and sometimes veal with chopped garlic, Romano cheese, eggs, breadcrumbs, a little olive oil and parsley. This is one case where Italy and Krebs have drifted apart.

On the other hand, the sausage in Krebs hasn't varied much at all over the years. But then, cured meats date back to the thirteenth century in the Mediterranean. Where they came from first is a matter of some debate. What can't be debated is that the practice of wives and maidens producing sausages in the home and selling or trading them within the village started long before any Italians arrived in Oklahoma's coal country. Family recipes date back over generations, reflecting the herbs and spices that grew naturally in their regions. Longtime Pittsburg County resident Marion Fassino said he gathers twice a year with friends to make hundreds of pounds of sausage.

"We go in on all the ingredients and share the labor so it don't cost us too much," said Fassino, who also mentioned he doesn't like fennel or sage in his sausage, but he doesn't hold it against anybody who does. Fassino said the tradition is simply an extension of the way he grew up in Pittsburg County.

"When we was kids, Daddy would get me and my brother in here in the kitchen every Sunday, and we'd make pasta."

---

7. Kate Whiteman, Jeni Wright and Angela Boggiano, *The Italian Kitchen Bible* (London: Hermes House, 2006), 12–13.

The Fassinos weren't alone in that practice, and the tradition was similar when it came time to make cheese. Italy is one of the world's foremost cheese producers, featuring a litany of styles and variations from practically every region. Some of the world's finest and most celebrated cheeses come from Lombardy, Veneto and Piedmont. Parmigiano-Reggiano has been a household name for years, with mozzarella, Asiago and Romano close behind. You probably have also heard of Fontina from the Aosta Valley, Gorgonzola and Italy's answer to cream cheese, mascarpone. If you've ever eaten an Italian deli sandwich, you've no doubt had provolone, and if you've ever had manicotti, you've eaten ricotta, whether you realize it or not. And if you haven't ever had the rich, semi-soft Taleggio, then you simply haven't lived. In Pittsburg County, the immigrants who came to coal country primarily made caciocavallo, a cow's milk cheese that's a household staple in southern Italy and Sicily. When young, it is mild in flavor and makes a great table cheese. When aged, it can be used grated in a variety of Italian dishes. That versatility made it perfect for the frontier lifestyle. Ironically, the family doing the best to continue the tradition of this primarily southern Italian cheese is the Lovera family, who hail from the north. But the Loveras helped prove Levenstein's theory of assimilation among Italians by eventually learning to master the art of caciocavallo in the 1990s after years of buying from local home cheese-makers.

Ask Joe Prichard or any of the other Krebs restaurateurs about the history of how lamb fries ended up on Krebs menus, and you'll get some interesting guesses. But the best guess as to how lamb fries made their way to these menus comes from the state of Oklahoma's grand dame of restaurants, Cattlemen's Steakhouse in Oklahoma City. David Egan is director of operations at Cattlemen's and a regular diner at Pete's Place. Egan and Joe Prichard have been friends for decades, even partnering to purchase fifty thousand pounds of lamb fries each year from Iceland. Egan's theory credits proximity to packing plants and a little luck for how lamb fries and/or Rocky Mountain oysters ended up on Cattlemen's menu back in the 1910s.

"Cattlemen's is in the Oklahoma City Stockyards, which is the still the largest feeder stockyards in the whole world, but from the 1910s through the 1970s, there were five major packing plants in the back of the Oklahoma City Stockyards," Egan explained. "However, the packing plants have basically moved outside of town because nobody wanted to live anywhere near them."

Egan went on to explain that during the time the packinghouses were close to Cattlemen's, then primarily a cafe, the packers used to toss testicles into the packing crates with steaks as waste byproduct.

Lamb fries are at the forefront of the fusion of prairie food with Old World Italian food at the Isle of Capri and three other restaurants in Pittsburg County.

"Then the cooks here would cut them up, batter-fry them and toss one on a plate as sort of a garnish," Egan said. "Pretty soon, people started requesting them. Today, lamb fries are our number one–selling appetizer."

But where did the idea come for how to cook them? Oklahoma's unofficial chef emeritus is John Bennett, who grew up on a cattle ranch near rural Healdton, Oklahoma, in the 1940s. Chef Bennett recalled gathering around a hot cauldron full of oil as the bulls were converted into steers during roundup. Bennett said freshly removed bits were tossed into a bucket, where a cook would find them, dredge them and toss them into the oil as the castration process continued—evidence that the consumption of testicles would've been well-established on the stomping grounds of so many head of cattle and livestock. Since Pete's Place served steaks as well as Italian fare at the same time Cattlemen's was in operation, it's very likely the practice of including discarded livestock testicles with steak deliveries was commonplace. Finding lamb fries on a menu in the early days of Pete's Place wouldn't have been at all disturbing to diners familiar with rural practices.

Steak and chicken were accepted fare at restaurants all over the country, dating back to the birth of restaurants in America. Their inclusion on the menu would've been partly to draw a broader range of customers and partly because of ease of availability. And just because Italians loved their ravioli and sausage doesn't mean they would turn their noses up at a good steak or freshly fried chicken.

But what beverage do you pair with this blend of bold flavors from the western Mediterranean and finger-licking goodness from the Western frontier—beer or wine? The answer is somewhere in between.

Chapter 3

CHOCTAW BEER

Scourge of the Indian Territory

By 1894, the coal-mining boom was hitting its stride in the Choctaw Nation. Trains bustled in and out of town, carrying coal to points in each direction. The workforce had bulged with the arrival of southern Italians and their families. Prosperity bred celebration and the spirits that come with it. Indian agents repeatedly took note of the liquor problem in reports to the Bureau of Indian Affairs, none more forcibly than Dew M. Wisdom, who wrote in 1894:

> *The sale of Choctaw beer, a drink compounded of barley, hops, tobacco, fishberries, and a small amount of alcohol, is manufactured without stint in many portions of this agency, especially in the mining communities. Many miners insist it is essential to their health, owing to the bad water usually found in mining camps, and they use it rather as a tonic or medicine than as a beverage, and this idea, that it is a proper tonic, is fostered and encouraged by some physicians. But it is somewhat remarkable as a fact in the scientific world that the water is always bad in the immediate mining centers, but good in the adjacent neighborhoods.*[8]

The Choctaws used fishberries as a paralyzing agent to disable fish, which would've made it particularly affecting. Recipes have evolved over more than a century of production, adding anything from oats, corn, malt, sugar

8. Stanley Clark, "Immigrants in the Choctaw Coal Industry," *Chronicles of Oklahoma* 33: 446.

and yeast. Regardless of the exact formula, Choctaw beer was easily made with ingredients "readily obtained at the grocery store" and, as the *Wilburton Gazette* noted on May 4, 1906, "can be prepared by any housewife."[9]

Miners excused their consumption of "Choc" thanks to poor water quality, claiming Choc had healing qualities. Local doctors commonly backed up their patients' claims, though perhaps because they were under the influence of Choc, too. A woman brought before the judge in Wilburton told the court she had made the beer under the advice of her doctor and showed the judge a doctor's note to prove it.[10]

Others argued that the water of the region was so laden with minerals that converting it into Choc beer was the only way to make it palatable. One newspaper in the town of Coalgate lent support to this claim by noting, "The water is so hard that when you want a drink you have to break off a piece."

Despite the efforts of the federal government to stop it, Choc beer production and consumption was so pervasive that it became known in the *Wilburton Gazette* in 1905 as the "territorial beverage" and in the *South McAlester Capital* in 1899 as the "national drink."[11]

Choc beer has nothing to do with chocolate and likely has little to do with the Choctaw Indian tribe for which it's named. There are those that will tell you Choc beer has little to do with beer at all. One thing is for sure, though: Choc is an enduring and still popular brew raised, if not born, in Pittsburg County. There is no record of its exact origins, but coal mining drew scores of men from all over Europe, including Germany and Belgium.

"The legend is that the Choctaw Indians that were native to the land taught the Italian immigrants to make beer," Joe Prichard said. "But I always kind of pictured some Belgian monk finding his way to the mines to minister to the miners and brewing up a batch of beer out of whatever he could get his hands on," Joe said. Joe's theory is given further credence in that the Choctaw hadn't even fully arrived from the Trail of Tears when coal mining began in southeastern Oklahoma.

A letter written by a young Frenchman named Joseph Lanchet on May 13, 1884, talks about the makeup of the peoples in coal country and describes their way of life:

> *About nine or ten miles from Atoka is the mining camp of Lehigh. All the coal dries I have seen in the Indian Territory, thus far, are in the Choctaw Nation. The country occupied by that tribe contains not only magnificent forests and fertile*

---

9. Steven L. Sewell, "Choctaw Beer: Tonic or Devil's Brew?" *Journal of Cultural Geography*, Spring/Summer 2006. Retrieved online.
10. Ibid.
11. Ibid.

prairies, where the grass grows five feet tall, but on the bosom of the earth there are incalculable mineral riches yet untouched. All the miners are white people and belong to several European nations. There are a good many Italians, a few Germans and Belgians, very few Frenchmen. A good workman earns from three to five dollars a day. That seems pretty good. But the miner is about the only member of his family, if he has one, that works, except when the boys get to be about twelve years old, then they begin to earn something themselves. Meanwhile the whole family lives on his sole earnings, and in these parts most of life's commodities are very high in price, higher than in France, except for meat. Raw meat, I mean, for when it is cooked it costs as much as in this old country; and to more effectively prevent him from growing rich there are frequent breakdowns, lock-outs, strikes, etc. Notwithstanding all this, an industrious, sober, prudent miner may save a little money, but I have not yet heard of anyone having got rich at this hard labor.

There is scant evidence of American Indians producing beer outside of the southwestern United States and practically none to indicate the Choctaw were skilled brewers. So the most likely origin of Choc beer is a motivated European immigrant with some experience in brewing beer who made a batch of the intoxicant and named it for the Choctaw Nation where he or she created it. If not a German or Belgian immigrant, the first Choc-maker could've come closer to North America. Among the first laborers in coal country were men shipped in from the West Indies, and the fact that some brewers sold a beverage called Jamaican Ginger that was code for Choc might mean the beverage came from the Caribbean. Most likely, the name has more to do with geography than cultural history. Regardless of its origin, Choc was a favorite among those within the mining communities in Oklahoma's coal country. The concoction could be brewed in a basement, garage, barn or kitchen and was the salvation of innumerable widows and maimed miners.

Like all beers, Choc is a fermentation of barley and hops. But that's where its relationship with standard beer ends. Zachary Prichard said the main difference between home-brewed Choc and the beer he brews at the Krebs Brewing Company is the barley.

"In normal beer brewing, the barley is malted," he said. "In homemade Choc, there is no malting."

Malting simulates the grain's natural germination cycle by wetting the barley kernels and allowing them to sprout. As the seedlings begin sprouting, the starchy insides of the kernels, called endosperm, begin to evolve and the hard, starchy endosperm begin to break down into natural malt sugars called maltose that brewers later liquefy during the mashing process. One of the important features of this process is the production of the enzymes brewers later use in the mashing process. The maltose sugars, along with proteins and dextrins, contribute the color, flavor, sweetness, body, mouthfeel and foam in the beer. From this process, brewers get barleymalt. Each grain of malted barley contains carbohydrates and enzymes that create the sugar, which ultimately determines the beer's alcohol content. Zach explained that because Choc wasn't malted, it couldn't be mashed with any efficiency, saying, "Choc was made with uncracked barley and steeped like tea in crocks with copious amounts of sugar added to increase the alcohol content level."

"I love Choc," said Sam Lovera. "When Dominca and I got married, we got five cases of Choc as a wedding gift." Sam didn't say whether that was his favorite wedding gift, but the smile on his face gave a pretty good indication as to where the gift stood in his memory.

Longtime Pittsburg County resident and Choc maker Marion Fassino said everyone makes it a little different. But Fassino's grandmother was a member of the infamous Fabrizzio family, still known today as the finest Choc makers in Pittsburg County. Fassino learned to make it watching his grandfather. He doesn't have a recipe written down; he makes it from memory.

"My grandpa, he made his different than what I make mine, Joe Prichard makes his. And really, the rest of the guys make it like I do."

How Fassino makes his is by first slow-cooking hops and barley. "We put the barley and hops in a muslin cloth and tie it off, some people might put a tough ol' ear of corn or maybe a little rice in there just to give a little different flavor."

Then Fassino attaches the bag of hops and barley to a stick and submerges it into a boiling pot of water, careful not to let it rest on bottom.

"I'll boil it on a slow roll for an hour and a half and cut the heat off," he said. Then he transfers the brew into a ten-gallon crock to let it cool to room temperature before adding sugar and yeast. The amount of sugar dictates how "spicy" the Choc will be.

"My father-in-law put about eight pounds of sugar to ten gallons of water," Fassino said. "That stuff would knock you on your tail."

Fassino said he likes his brew mellow enough to allow him to enjoy the day.

"I use five or six pounds of sugar to ten gallons of water," Fassino said. "Then I won't mess with it for a day or two. I'll put a pillowcase over it and tie it off, listen to it—you can hear that yeast workin'. Maybe check in on it now and then."

Fassino says by the third day, the yeast stops working.

"And you'd better have your bottles ready, because if you wait too long you'll have vinegar."

Fassino said you then add a small amount of sugar into the bottle, fill it with beer and cap it. After a few more days of rest, the Choc is ready to be uncapped, and don't be surprised if you get a puff of blue smoke.

"You see that blue smoke come off it, and you know you're drinking a good Choc beer," said Dominica Lovera.

A 2006 article entitled, "Choctaw Beer: Tonic or Devil's Brew?" in the *Journal of Cultural Geography* by Steven Sewell, includes a collection of snippets from the many newspapers in Oklahoma's coal country indicating the trials, tribulations and folly brought on by the consumption of Choc beer and the quandary it posed on law enforcement. In fact, newspapers at the time hint that local law enforcement offered substance to the adage that one should join a movement you cannot defeat.

On May 24, 1895, the *Hartshorne Sun* declared that "a pint is a pound the world around, but if it is Choctaw beer it more nearly approximates a ton."

A new United States court came to South McAlester in 1894, and thirty-four of about two hundred criminal cases on the first docket in January were for selling or introducing "spirituous liquors" into Indian Territory. Much legal wrangling ensued over whether or not Choc was an intoxicating liquor. Marshals continued to raid establishments selling "malt drinks." The South McAlester court overflowed with cases of illegal liquor sales. The *South McAlester Capital* noted on December 8, 1899, "Judge Clayton rightly looks upon Choctaw beer as an intoxicant and he proposes to eliminate it if possible from the economy."[12]

Sentences weren't terribly prohibitive. Many violators received the minimum sentence of thirty days and a one-dollar fine, which was less than tax would've been. But not everyone got off so light. When Frank Pardon was sentenced in 1899 for manufacturing Choc, the *South McAlester Capital* reported that "he that drinketh corn tea because the water was bad" will "rusticate" for ninety-one days in the Fort Smith jail.[13]

Choc makers continued to use health as an explanation for their activities. In June 1900, a Mrs. Quinn of Coalgate was caught with a fresh keg of Choc. A report in the *Coalgate Courier* indicated that Mrs. Quinn told authorities she had brewed the beer for her sick daughter and that the numerous men at the house were doctors visiting her ailing daughter. No arrests were made, but the deputy did take down the names of the "doctors," whom he suspected were practicing medicine without a license from the Choctaw Medical Board. The *South McAlester Review* tried to explain all the beer-drinking by reprinting an article first published in the *North American Review*

---

12. Ibid.
13. Ibid.

that contended beer drinking was driven by a craving for the "elements left out in the manufacture of white bread."[14]

Over time, law enforcement officers began to reap financial benefits themselves thanks to the Choctaw beer industry. Fines brought in considerable revenue. Sewell noted that records of court proceedings began to look more like account ledgers than legal records. Income derived from fines and court costs poured into government coffers.[15]

Pittsburg County became so notorious for its libations that it drew the attention of radical prohibitionist Carry Nation, who held a rally in Hartshorne in 1905. Of Nation's visit, the Sayre, Oklahoma periodical *Headlight Journal* remarked, "The curious will have an opportunity to see her and to procure one of her hatchets."

A 1907 editorial in the *Wilburton Gazette* hinted that corruption played a role in these activities when it declared, "When a Deputy Marshall [*sic*] accepts a bribe of $10 per month from an old Polish woman for making Choc and through a mistake she gives him $20, he should either give $10 of it back or issue a permit for another month." In a similar comment, the *Gazette* noted, "If the Choctaw beer makers should go on strike for thirty days the Deputy Marshals would all starve out."

The Great Depression increased production as suddenly everyone was out of work except for those brewing Choc, which had carried so many financially desperate people through hard times in the coal belt. In 1933, the Twenty-first Amendment repealed federal prohibition, but Oklahoma remained a dry state until 1959. However, a law was passed to allow the sale of beer with no more 3.2 percent alcohol content, which is still in effect today, though a movement toward reform of state alcohol laws is afoot.

Italian food and Choc beer had proven so popular during Pittsburg County's coal mining boom that it was inevitable someone would combine the two to make a business. What wasn't inevitable was someone making a business that would not only outlast the coal boom but zip past the Y2K scare as well. Even more farfetched was the idea of Italian immigrants in Indian Territory. Pittsburg County's Italian population isn't what it used to be, but it's still very strong. While terms like *fuhgeddaboutit* are stereotypes assigned to Italian Americans thanks to their primary depiction as East Coasters, the Italians in Pittsburg County speak with a twang and drawl thicker than the four shades of green that thatch its rolling hills. The twang still echoes through Pittsburg County, and the Choc still flows. But both would likely be a barely recalled memory if southeastern Oklahoma hadn't been home to enormous deposits of the world's foremost energy source at the time.

14. Ibid.
15. Ibid.

Chapter 4

"SEEKING BREAD, THEY FOUND THE GRAVE"

They didn't speak English. They prayed thanksgiving and forgiveness via the Catholic church in a land ruled by heathens and Protestants. Italians endured discrimination and oppressive working conditions to subsist in Pittsburg County. But that's what the hungry do, especially when lured by financial freedom. The Italian food tradition of Krebs is the heart of the food history of Pittsburg County, but civilization came to the hills at the feet of the Ouachita Mountains for one thing and one thing only: black coal.

Containing a tarlike substance called bitumen, bituminous coal is between lignite and anthracite in quality. It is the result of high pressure exerted on lignite. It was formed in the hills of southeastern Oklahoma eons ago and remained undetected, or at least unrecognized for its value, until political turmoil halfway around the world for one of Italy's neighbors fortified the westward push of Western civilization in the New World.

But before any boat ever bumped against the shores of North America, the native peoples of Oklahoma lived a transient life, moving with the seasons to avoid harsh, unpredictable weather. The native peoples, in this regard, were far wiser than the state's current residents. There is evidence of tribal life in southeastern Oklahoma that dates back to the Paleolithic period, but it wasn't until a Frenchman sent on a mission to save the mother country's broken economy set foot in a murky creek that earth's richest energy resource at the time was recognized by someone who understood its worth.

Sent to this land of savages with nothing less than the salvation of his homeland at stake, this explorer knew right away he might well have discovered the antidote to France's terminally ill economy, which was on life support after years of spending that King Louis XIV committed to wine, women and war. Louis was good at all those expensive habits, so he died in glory at seventy-two but left his son to face the bankruptcy of their nation on his own. When Louis XIV died in 1715, the country needed new ideas for generating revenue. Enter John Law, a Scotch economist with savant-like tendencies for calculation and projection. Law was hired as controller general of finances of France under young King Louis XV and quickly looked across the pond for financial opportunity—namely, to the Mississippi delta.

Bernard de la Harpe was one of the charges who followed Law's purview west, traveling to Louisiana as a result of Law's scheme of settling Louisiana.[16] La Harpe was made commandant among the Nassonites, Cadodaquious, Nadacos and Natchitoches tribes and sent forth to explore the Red River, learn about the savages in that region, establish posts among the Cadodaquious and do all in his power to establish trade with the Spanish, who were entrenched in Texas and New Mexico.

On August 13, 1719, La Harpe's expedition crossed the Arkansas-Oklahoma border near Grassy Lake and eventually set up camp southwest of Bokhoma. Surviving on buffalo and roebucks that had to be smoked or cured for fear the intense Oklahoma heat would ruin the meat, La Harpe and company continued over hills and across prairies, where they found slate quarries and several pieces of rock crystal as they wound through the Ouachita Mountains. On September 2, 1719, they crossed a great prairie with two streams winding through the thicket. It was in this vicinity that La Harpe found many deposits abundant with coal in and around a small stream now called Coal Creek.

La Harpe believed he'd found the key to trade leverage with Spain on this prairie, and he said, "There is not in the whole colony of Louisiana an establishment more useful to make than on the branch of this river not only because of the mild climate, the fertility of the land, the richness of the minerals, but also because of the possibility of trade that one might introduce with Spain and New Mexico. If one could control the trade which the Spanish carry on with the Padoucas and Arricaras, one could become master of this region."

But fate had a different plan. Law's scheme to leverage the perceived success of his Mississippi Company with investor fervor and the wealth of its Louisiana prospects into a sustainable joint-trading company would implode at the end of 1720, and Law was fired by Philippe d'Orléans, regent of

---

16. Anna Lewis, "La Harpe's First Expedition in Oklahoma," *Chronicles of Oklahoma* 2, no. 4 (December 1924): 331.

France for Louis XV. La Harpe's explorations ended in November 1719 without any trading partners. He returned to France in January 1720 but returned to North America by the end of the year and reaped no success. He would return to the Arkansas River in 1722 for further exploration and be credited with discovering Little Rock, Arkansas. He also stopped off in Pensacola, Florida, to preside over its transfer to the Spanish before returning to France in 1723 to write his memoirs, which included his coal findings in southeastern Oklahoma.

La Harpe was the first man from the civilized world to happen onto the coal-rich hills of southeastern Oklahoma, but he was far from the last. As coal grew in value, prospectors scoured the countryside for it and began arriving not long after the Civil War. So, too, did a new Indian tribe. The indigenous peoples would have to make room for an influx of fifteen thousand Choctaw Indians, who arrived from the Deep South on the Trail of Tears, starting in 1830 and continuing with varying degrees of intensity through 1903. These rolling green hills teeming with natural resources would become the Choctaw Nation of Oklahoma.

About 120 years after La Harpe traipsed among the tribal peoples of Oklahoma and Arkansas, James J. McAlester[17] was born in Sebastian, Arkansas. He was raised in Fort Smith and later volunteered his services to the Confederate army at the outbreak of the Civil War, rising to the rank of captain. When the war ended, McAlester took up studies back in Fort Smith and bunked with Oliver Weldon, a former engineer who had surveyed Indian Territory to the west. Weldon, who had worked for the U.S. Geological Survey mapping Indian Territory before the war, shared with McAlester a memorandum book detailing vast coal fields at the Crossroads area in Indian Territory. Only twenty-four, McAlester left school for the Indian Territory, where, after a stint working for the trading firm of Harlan and Rooks, he found a job with the Reynolds and Hannaford Trading Company. He quickly convinced its owners to locate a general store in the town of Tupelo in the Choctaw Nation. Hearing of railroad plans to extend through Indian Territory and knowing that rich deposits of coal were in an area north of the town of Perryville, McAlester convinced Reynolds and Hannaford that Bucklucksy would be a more suitable and profitable location for the trading post. McAlester constructed a trading post/general store at that location in late 1869. The general store was an immediate success, but J.J. McAlester recognized an even greater opportunity in the abundance of coal deposits in the area and began obtaining rights to the coal deposits from

17. Paul Nesbitt, "J.J. McAlester," *Chronicles of Oklahoma* 11 (June 1933).

the Choctaws in anticipation of the impending construction of a rail line through Indian Territory.

By virtue of having been the first to extend its line to the northern border of Indian Territory, the Union Pacific Railway Southern Branch earned right of way and a liberal bonus of land to extend the line to Texas. A number of New York businessmen, including Levi P. Morton, Levi Parsons, August Belmont, J. Pierpont Morgan, George Denison and John D. Rockefeller, were interested in extending the rail line through Indian Territory, and the Missouri-Kansas-Texas Railroad, familiarly called the Katy Railroad, began its corporate existence in 1865 toward that end. Morton and Parsons selected a site near the Kansas border with Indian Territory at which a town operated by the railroad could be located, with the settlement incorporated under the name of Parsons, Kansas, in 1871.

That same year, J.J. McAlester, after buying out Reynolds's share of the trading post, journeyed with a sample of coal to Parsons and begged an audience with railroad officials. Given the chance, McAlester waxed poetic about the superior nature of Oklahoma coal, which along with the congressional subsidies attached to coal mining made the decision easy for the good folks of Parsons to locate a line near his store at Bucklucksy, arriving in 1872 at which point Katy Railroad officials named the railway stop McAlester.

On August 22, 1872, J.J. McAlester married Rebecca Burney, who was a member of the Chickasaw Nation, and this made it possible for McAlester to gain citizenship and the right to own property in both the Choctaw and Chickasaw nations. This allowed McAlester to legally obtain his own mineral rights to the coal deposits. McAlester quickly obtained land near the intersection of the north–south and east–west rail line intersection, where he opened a second general store and was able to continue doing business selling coal to the railroads.

The Choctaw Coal and Railway, an east–west rail line that ran through the coal mining district at Krebs and connected with the north–south line at McAlester, was built in 1888, but McAlester couldn't agree on the issue of right of way with its ownership. The Choctaw Coal and Railway subsequently purchased land to the south of McAlester's general store, creating a natural trading crossroads where the two rail lines crossed and quickly became a bustling community designated as South McAlester. The original town location became known familiarly as North McAlester or North Town although early U.S. census records simply identified it as McAlester. The two towns operated as separate communities until 1907.

Coal mining drew all sorts to the Indian Territory, which quickly necessitated someone to wield the sword of justice. The man chosen was a judge of mixed blood named Edmond Fulsom Krebs. The town that bore his name was such a major cog in the local coal industry that it nearly became Pittsburg County's seat instead of McAlester. Little is known about Edmond Krebs, and there was some dispute as to whether the town was named after him. A doctor named Jim Krebs was also well known at the time, but Steve DeFrange of the Krebs Heritage Museum said Edmond Krebs was the man whom the town's name honors.

Oklahoma's coal industry prospered through the 1920s. Production rose from one million tons to two million between 1891 and 1901 and leapt to three million tons by 1903. Production peaked at four million tons during World War I, but oil began cutting into the value of coal in the early 1920s, and it would never regain its previous value. And so Pittsburg County felt its own mini-depression before the Great Depression began, triggering an exodus of its residents, many of whom would return when the Great Depression hammered the rest of the country through the 1930s.

The coal boom; however, needed something more than deep pockets to finance it: it needed men to mine the resource, men desperate for work and willing to risk their lives to support their families. And those men were found mostly in depressed European countries like Scotland, Ireland, Wales and Italy, places where opportunities were so few that the very real risk of death, as exemplified by more than three thousand deaths in the mines during the boom, was simply an escape from a slow death by starvation. As one writer of the time noted, "Seeking bread, they found the grave."[18] It also drew heavily from Poland and Russia. The Italians were last to arrive to Pittsburg County but came in the greatest numbers. By the time they arrived, many of the other European immigrants had scattered farther west on the coal belt into neighboring Oklahoma counties and on down into northwest Texas. Initially, the mining companies preferred workers who didn't speak English, thinking it would prevent them from joining the fast-growing movement of labor organization.[19] But those who mistake a language barrier for a lack of good sense are almost always proven wrong. The Italians adapted quickly to the movement and soon were running it.

Not every family came to work in the mines, and those who did work in the mines usually sought a way out as soon as possible. Those who found

18. Stanley Clark, "Immigrants in the Choctaw Coal Industry," *Chronicles of Oklahoma* 33:447.
19. Ibid., 442.

their way out of the mines almost invariably made a living in the food and beverage trade, whether baking, butchering, producing cheese and sausage, importing native foods, bottling soda pop, distilling illegal spirits or brewing illegal beer. So when the succession of wild economic spikes and collapses began and the population fluctuated, the food culture remained rock solid. Dozens of Italian names appear on the old business registers as owners of bakeries, meat markets, grocery stores and cafes. But three families in particular came to the Choctaw Nation around the turn of the nineteenth century, and their legacies continue today: the Giacomos, Loveras and Piegaris.

Steve DeFrange, curator of the Krebs Heritage Museum, said the hills of Pittsburg County are still rich with coal today, but in the years since the resource fell out of favor, the southeastern Oklahoma coal has been found to be too high in sulfur for mining.

Coal was the bait to lure people to the area, but like so many boom industries, its bubble eventually burst. Unlike many coal-mining communities, Pittsburg County was able to adjust, dust itself off and develop sustainable income in other industries. This helped keep the county's culinary curators in place and pave the way for a few well-established families to cook their way into the hearts and minds of folks all around. Along the way, key political figures and strokes of economic good fortune found their way to Pittsburg County. And while no one can say good luck befell the area because of the food, neither is anyone going to tell you it didn't hurt to have several great places to eat when hosting dignitaries who would be responsible for that good fortune coming its way.

Chapter 5

LESSONS LEARNED

In a four-thousand-square-foot warehouse adjacent to the legendary yellow house that is Pete's Place in Krebs, owner Joe Prichard, his son Zachary, brewmeister Mike Lalli and two others are trying to solve a problem with a beer shipment. It's a problem few restaurateurs have, but Pete's Place isn't like many restaurants.

Pete's was opened in 1925 by Joe's grandfather, Pietro Piegari, who not only established the business that would sustain four generations of his family but also decided Pietro Piegari wasn't a suitable name and changed his name to Pete and the family name to Prichard.

That name has now produced four generations and two restaurants that have combined to serve family recipes for more than 120 years. The secret to success for Pete Prichard and the family that's followed is sticking to what they know for close to 90 years, so the food is almost effortless, which allows them to concentrate on service and growth.

"There isn't anything unique about our menu," Joe Prichard said. "What's unique is the style we use to deliver it. We serve family style."

That means community tables and food served in bowls or dishes with empty plates for everyone in the party. The food was never fancy and won't claim to be now: pasta, traditional red sauce derived from an old family recipe, grilled steaks, fried chicken and shrimp, chicken Parmesan, ravioli and lamb fries like you'll find at Oklahoma City's centenarian steakhouse Cattlemen's, though Prichard is quick to point out that while they source the fries from the same place, those at Pete's are better.

"We cut ours a little different," Prichard said. "I think ours are a little better."

Joe said he didn't really know when Pete's Place started serving them, but it's been as long as he's been alive, and a menu on the wall that looks to be from the early 1960s bears that claim out.

The ravioli comes from a recipe brought over from the Old Country by Prichard's grandfather, who helped make them by hand in his restaurant for more than four decades. Today, the ravioli are still made in-house, but high-volume demand requires the help of a machine Joe had built especially to press the dough around the pork filling.

"Ours are different than most," Prichard explained. "We use all-purpose flour and semolina. People either love them or hate them. There's not much of a dividing line."

Served under that same traditional red sauce, the doughy raviolis are almost dumplings. Pete's also serves them toasted. Either way, they're highly addictive. If you sit for any kind of spell, the plate has no chance at returning to the kitchen with anything on it.

While sausage, spaghetti and meatballs, ravioli, steaks, chicken and lamb fries highlight the menu, it's beer that might well be the magic potion that saved not only the Prichard family but every family in Krebs. In 1919, Pete started brewing and selling out of the same house where Pete's Place still stands today. The beer was called Choc, an homage to the Choctaw Nation, where it became popular, and Choc is the name Joe and Zachary put on each outgoing bottle of beer from the brewery they built next to Pete's Place in 1996. And it's the label that is the problem with this outgoing batch of the brewery's newest batch due to go out to Shelton Brothers in Massachusetts, which plans to distribute the new brew to thirty-eight states, Brazil and several countries in Europe.

"It was too wet when you put the labels on," Zachary says to his dad.

Joe isn't used to being on this side of a correction, and he's not too comfortable with it. He reaches into one of the open boxes, extracts a bottle and runs his fingers along the custom label that reads Prairie Ale.

"Yeah, it's still pretty wet," he says with a hint of resignation. Joe isn't the kind of guy who relishes pointing out others' mistakes, but neither does he hesitate to miss a teaching opportunity colored with his trademark sarcasm. But since it's clear his decision to label and pack bottles a little too early was a misstep, he's forthright and magnanimous.

"Yeah," he sighs. "It's a lesson learned."

Joe Prichard is the third-generation owner of Pete's Place whose expansion in 1994 increased capacity and allows the restaurants to serve as many as two thousand people on weekends. And it was his idea to turn Choc beer into a brand the family could introduce around the world. But he's not the first owner of Pete's Place to build on lessons learned through mistakes, accidents and miscalculations.

The first and most important mistake Pete Prichard made was thinking he was a coal miner. It was an easy mistake to make as he was born to a coal-miner-to-be on June 29, 1895, in San Gregorio Magno in the Campania region of southern Italy. His father's name was Luca Piegari, and he hadn't yet set foot in a coal mine when his son Pietro was born that summer day. All Piegari knew was that he had another mouth to feed in a village bereft of business opportunity and too many hands to work the local olive trees. The mountainous area of Campania offered precious little farmland. So in 1902, Piegari followed many of his compatriots to the United States, where coal mining opportunities abounded. Like everyone else, Luca landed first in New York City, but worked his way west. Established Italian communities drew a great number of immigrants west to Chicago and St. Louis. Luca followed those crowds, but he eventually ventured even farther west through Wyoming and Denver before landing in the tiny town of Krebs, Oklahoma. The first coal miners in Oklahoma came mostly from Pennsylvania, which was a hotbed for English, Irish, Scotch and Welsh immigrants. Their familiarity with the rising labor movement made mine owners in Oklahoma uneasy. A few Italians were in the initial group and were preferred by the mining companies because of their inability to communicate with English-speaking coworkers. Some were even paid to return to their homeland to convince friends and family to join them under contract in the mines.

Krebs was a magnet for Italians, though they settled in other parts of coal country, too. Luca Piegari followed his countrymen to Oklahoma, landing first in Hartshorne before likely bouncing around Haileyville, Carbon and maybe even Lehigh before summoning his family a year later. The rocky hillsides of Krebs weren't too unlike San Gregorio, and the Italian population quickly established traditions from the homeland, including the formation of a musical band called the Christopher Columbus Mutual Aid Society.

Conditions were miserable in the Choctaw Nation, where the hours were long and backbreaking, not too mention dangerous. Coal veins ranged from four to two feet in height, meaning miners spent most of their work days stooped or on their knees, often in standing water. Some miners were paid by the ton, but extracted rocks and soil were sifted out. While the work was lucrative in the context of the miner's other options, work could be sporadic and weather conditions could limit opportunity. Companies in the past often paid in script and set up company housing and stores, which, in some cases, put workers in indentured servitude. But by the time Luca Piegari arrived, reform had begun and competition had grown to where conditions slowly improved.

The growing community of Italians eight-year-old Pietro Piegari joined in Pittsburg County was hardworking and socially active with no intention of losing the customs of home. And for Italians, that means food. Back home in southern Italy, it wasn't uncommon to subsist on minestrone, bread and wine. Oklahoma offered more livestock, so sausage and cheese were made in practically every home. The beverage of choice, though, was not wine but Choc beer.

When little Pietro Piegari arrived in this land of cheese, sausage and home-brewed libations, he showed an early proclivity for cooking, helping his mother in the kitchen whenever he could. It wasn't uncommon for him to make off with a frying pan or other cooking implement to cook up whatever quarry he and his fellow junior hunters had bagged.

While the economy in Krebs was far better than back home, it wasn't uncommon for mining work to be limited to about two hundred days a year due to weather and other impediments. To make ends meet, children were often called upon to hustle up extra money any way they could. The charismatic Pietro was so good at hustling money by clever means that he quit school after the fourth grade, finishing what amounted to a year and a half of formal education. Children were often hired by the mines to reach spots inaccessible to adult miners. Pietro recognized this opportunity and went for it, even changing his named to Pete Prichard to gain an advantage in finding work.

Pete Prichard followed the line of men into the mines off and on for more than decade, working long hours and finding post-shift respite in the homes of widows who sold food and drink to weary miners. As he got old enough to travel, he made his way to Arkansas, where he worked several months on the railroad. During that time, he got some cooking lessons from Greek immigrants that would serve him the rest of his life.[20] But it was back in Pittsburg County, now living in Krebs, in 1916 where Pete learned he was not destined to stay a miner when a cave-in crushed his leg.

The mines were marked by disasters that cost thousands of lives. In the Krebs Heritage Museum, there is a light-blue ledger two inches thick filled with the names of those who died in the mines around Krebs and McAlester. There were numerous ways miners could lose their lives in the underground or shaft mines. Rockfalls, "windy shots," coal dust blasts and noxious gases were only a few of the dangers they faced, not to mention the residual effects that caused black lung. By the 1880s, the phrase "killed by a windy shot" was

20. Kenny Brown, *The Italians in Oklahoma* (Norman: University of Oklahoma Press, 1980), 38.

Pete's Place has grown exponentially since its opening in 1925. *Courtesy of the Prichard family.*

common in mining reports. When a miner used too much black powder or improperly tamped down a charge before setting off an explosion, "windy shots" spewed sparks into the mine and ignited methane gas, coal dust or both. The resulting blast could travel through miles of tunnels and kill or maim miners far from where the explosion was ignited.

Pete was lucky not to end up in the blue ledger, but like so many others who barely survived the mine, he lost a significant means of revenue. Now married to Pasqualina Choch, who would bear him four children, Pete had to hearken back to his days of hustling for money since he had so little formal education on which to lean. He'd learned to cook Italian comfort food and brew Choctaw beer, but he was born to sell the sizzle. So cook and sell is what Pete Prichard did to support his family. He had no other options.

"Back then you didn't have any workmen's comp or social security," said Lovera's Grocery Store and Meat Market owner Sam Lovera, whose family history follows a similar narrative. "My aunt Mary told me when my grandfather and uncle were killed in the mines, the Red Cross showed up with a box of canned goods to help feed the kids and that was it."

Back in 1916, Choc was well established, which is why Pete Prichard had no problem learning to make and sell it starting in 1919. While he didn't invent the practice, he certainly perfected it.

"I don't know why his beer got more popular than others," Joe Prichard said. "Maybe he had a card game going on at his place or something like that. What I do know is he started brewing in the basement, and it was extremely popular.

"When I was a little kid, they were still brewing in the basement of the restaurant and bottling it. But we were pretty small. We'd siphon the beer out of the vats into bottles with a little sugar in the bottom, and we'd put the cap on it and all that kind of stuff just by hand."

Pete wasn't the first person to use food and drink as a means to survive. In fact, even women like Minnie Peccio who weren't widowed sold dried salami sandwiches to the miners to supplement the family income. This is where Pete's God-given ability as a host came in handy. Whether it was a card game or Pete's gregarious personality and natural showmanship that initially lured in customers, Pete recognized that profits would increase as the menu did. The men that came to Pete's place for beer were as hungry as they were thirsty.

"My granddad opened up his home to the miners when they'd come out of the mines in the evenings to drink the beer, and he saw them bringing cold cuts

The interior at Minnie's Italian Dinners in the early days. *Courtesy of the Peccio family.*

and cheeses and stuff like that to eat with the beer," Joe said. "He figured out relatively quickly that he could sell them some of those food items."

Pretty soon, Pete was selling whatever cheese, sausage or bread he could make or buy cheaply to pair with his Choc. If a chicken were available, he would butcher and fry it. Whatever could be converted into profit, Pete prepared with aplomb, and his reputation as a cook became legendary. Business quickly increased as miners and neighbors would come over to Pete's "place" to eat, drink and make merry.

Pete's Place officially opened for business in 1925 in a spare room in what was then a small house. The business still runs in that home today. In the early days, the house sat alone, barely visible thanks to a thicket of trees that surrounded it, on a dirt-and-gravel street just off the road into Krebs. Soon, the family's quarters moved into an upstairs addition, while downstairs, Pete served a menu that reflected the surivivalist spirit of both Italy and rural America: ravioli, spaghetti, sausage, cheese and tomato sauce, meatballs, chicken, steak, and lamb fries. But the money was made by selling Choc in the basement. Legend had it the beer was made in a bathtub.

Pietro Piegari changed his name to Pete Prichard and then turned his family's home in a quiet spot on a dirt road in Pittsburg County into Pete's Place in 1925.

"The funny thing about it is there is a bathtub in the basement," Joe Prichard said. "But it isn't where the beer was made. There were a couple of crocks where the Choc was made, but the tub was down there."

That bathtub still resides in the basement, but hasn't held a bath in years. Joe said he remembered his father, Bill, going down to the basement during the summer, drawing a cool bath where he would soak a bit to cool off before taking a nap on the cot against the east wall. Joe said Choc was most likely brewing and possibly being sipped while his father bathed, but it was never actually made in the bathtub.

John Shields, who worked at Pete's Place as a manager for about one year back in the early 1960s, said, "Everybody knew when they heard that door slam he was done napping and you'd better get back to work." Shields would go on to make his own contribution to Pittsburg County's culinary history with Shields Drive-In the 1960s.

Joe Prichard said it's impossible to know exactly what his grandfather offered the day he opened.

"For a long time, the daily menu was posted on a chalkboard," he said. "And it usually only had four things on it."

But Pete's Place does have a framed menu from decades ago hanging on the wall. It's undated but appears to be from the 1960s, listing a Regular Dinner with chicken or lamb fries (both of which would've been batter-fried) for seventy-five cents, which would've included pasta with sauce and salad prepared with imported olive oil. The Ravioli Dinner was fifty cents, as was the Spaghetti Dinner, which included meatballs. The ravioli served then and today at Pete's Place is stuffed with sausage and covered in tomato sauce.

The food at Pete's Place reflects the evolution of the Italian palate, including its adaption to the hills and prairies of southeastern Oklahoma. Joe Prichard said that his grandfather's recipes are absolutely authentic to southern Italy circa 1925, but the way he served them isn't necessarily the way they would've been served in Italy.

"You're not going to find spaghetti and meatballs served in Italy," Joe Prichard said. "You'll find spaghetti, meatballs and sauce but not necessarily served on the same plate."

Prichard said the other big difference between how food is served in Italy versus the United States is the amount of sauce and the texture of the pasta.

"We over-sauce and overcook pasta here by Italian standards," Prichard laughed. "But the way we serve our food at Pete's Place is the way it's been served since 1925."

The big ticket at Pete's Place was the Dinner Complete, which included ravioli, spaghetti and all the trimmings for a whopping seven dollars. Joe said that would've simply been a family dinner that included all of the Italian specialties, plus bread and salad. The menu also included the Dutch Lunch Plate, which is simply an antipasto plate.

Under Steak Dinners, the menu offers T-bone steak for seventy-five cents or a larger T-bone for ninety cents. Sirloins were sold for a dollar and a half or a dollar and seventy-five cents, doubtlessly serving two or four people. For a quarter, diners could get an order of imported olives, a loaf of toasted garlic bread, a Salima Sandwich, Cheese Sandwich Bake Ham Sandwich or order of anchovies. Chicken sandwiches were thirty-five cents.

There was another section of the menu that most likely indicates an attempt to draw more than just the Italians into Pete's Place. Lebanese immigrants who arrived in Oklahoma not long after the Italians established a number of "Lebanese steakhouses" from Tulsa to Oklahoma City and Bristow in between, which served steaks and chops with authentic Lebanese mezzes like tabouleh, hummus and baba ghanoush starting in the 1940s and continuing today. The inclusion of steak and fried chicken on the menu was partially an attempt to draw outside the Italian community but also part of the Italian tradition of using local ingredients. The decision to keep the same menu today is also out of tradition.

The menu on the wall at Pete's Place proves how little has changed over the years while presenting a clue to the good-natured outlaw spirit of southeastern Oklahoma. Oklahoma never ratified the Twenty-first Amendment in 1933. It wasn't until 1959 when the state legislature made an amendment to the Oklahoma Constitution that established package stores where spirits, classified as any beverage with more than 3.2 percent alcohol by volume, could be sold at state-controlled prices. Bars

Pete Prichard behind the stove at Pete's Place. *Courtesy of the Prichard family.*

and restaurants were left with beer that fell below 3.2 percent alcohol content, leading to what was called "liquor by the wink." Pittsburg County's disdain for liquor laws was legendary. The old menu framed in the halls of Pete's Place lists bottles of beer for ten and fifteen cents, along with coffee and milk for a nickel and Coca-Cola or pop on ice for five cents. What's curious is the cost of ginger ale, which is listed for twenty-five cents a pint and forty cents a quart with ice. The fact that the ginger ale was five times more expensive than soda pop and ten cents more than beer might indicate it had an ingredient with higher octane than sugar, syrup and carbonated water. The price could indicate that ginger ale was served with something more than ice or it could reference a concoction called "Jamaica ginger," which soon was "being sold and drank" throughout Indian Territory, according the March 24, 1992 edition of the *Indian Chieftan*.[21] And Jamaica ginger was code for Choctaw Beer.

Of all the food and drink served at Pete's Place and any other cafe or restaurant in Krebs, Choc beer was easily the most profitable item on the menu. He might've sold more steak, chicken and lamb fries, but those items had to be taxed. Because Choc was illegal, it also went unreported and was thus practically pure profit.

While there are some records that claim Pete also made wine, his grandson highly doubts the validity.

"Did he sell wine? I have no doubt that he did. But grapes don't grow too good around here," Joe said. "There's places not too far from here where you can grow grapes, and I know my grandfather wouldn't have hesitated to sell it. But whatever wine was being sold here was most probably made by somebody else."

There is no doubt Pete was making and selling Choc. Whether it was his recipe or salesmanship, Pete's name became synonymous with it and eventually drew the attention of local law enforcement. In April 1932, Pete was convicted of being in possession of sixty-four quarts and ten gallons of Choc beer and subsequently served a short prison sentence.

Joe recalls his father talking about how as the years passed, the local law enforcement became friendlier and would alert his father and his grandfather of busts.

"They would tell them they were coming and to leave a little out for them to confiscate to satisfy their superiors," Joe said through a wry smile it's hard to imagine he didn't come by honestly. Joe also recalled that part of the arrangement between local law enforcement and his grandfather included some command performances.

---

21. Sewell, "Choctaw Beer."

The Prichards get to work. *Courtesy of the Prichard family.*

Families have been dining at Pete's Place since 1925. *Courtesy of the Prichard family.*

Pete Prichard tended to work in the kitchen more as he got older. *Courtesy of the Prichard family.*

"When the Pittsburg County Sheriff's family would come to town for the holidays, or something like that, he would come and arrest my granddad and put him in jail so he'd have to cook for his family."

Law enforcement wasn't the only obstacle Pete Prichard faced. In the early years of World War II, while Japanese Americans were being interned during World War II, first-generation citizens from nations like Germany and Italy were not allowed to possess weapons, which included knives. So, Pete's Place had to negotiate dinner service without knives. During Christmas, Pete was known to open the restaurant after midnight mass for those who'd attended.

"I have fond memories of my grandfather," Joe said. "He was bigger than life, and he loved people almost as much as he loved to cook."

Pete was meticulous about the quality of food that he served and was known to shut the restaurant down for weeks at a time if he couldn't source quality ingredients. But as the coal boom intensified, industrious immigrants started venturing out of the mines and into business themselves.

Chapter 6

OUT OF THE MINES, INTO THE FOOD INDUSTRY

In the Krebs Heritage Museum, there is reference to a 1905 visit by Adolfo Rossi, an emigration official from Italy, who reported that Italians operated half a dozen grocery and general stores in Krebs. A 1911 report by the United States Senate's Immigration Commission also testified to the small groceries, bakeries and restaurants opened in Krebs. Oklahoma business directories from the 1910s show that Italians owned numerous stores, with meat markets, bakeries and cafes among the most common concepts. It's no surprise that, outside of coal mining, the most common occupations among Italian immigrants revolved around food. Long before Italy was united in the early nineteenth century, the cuisine was in development for a good 1,400 years prior and was influenced by various post–Roman Empire invasions by its Mediterranean neighbors. France, Greece and the Middle Eastern world took turns colonizing and abandoning Italy through the centuries after Rome fell, each time leaving behind flavors and cooking techniques that came to create what we now know as Italian cuisine.

Food proved to be a reliable revenue stream for Italian peasants, either as a primary or secondary source of income. But like any industry, it is demand-driven. And demand for food fluctuates wildly with the state of a local economy. People must eat to survive, but when wealth and vigorous trade arise so, too, does general consumption. Ingredient-stretching dishes like minestrone go back to being a small part of a meal and make way for the spoils of whatever can be imported and implemented with the rich resources of the local agriculture. Before oil began making coal irrelevant and subsequently dampening the economy, the locals in Pittsburg County developed a taste for imported Italian ingredients.

According to Kenny Brown's *The Italians in Oklahoma*, Giusseppe Fassino arrived in Krebs with his brother Giovanni in 1896 at the age of thirty-three. Born in Canischio in the province of Turin, Fassino quit school to work as a shepherd after turning ten. He migrated to France and then Switzerland, where he worked on the St. Gotthard Tunnel in the Alps. After being drafted by the Italian military in 1883, Fassino went home to serve three years.

While the north appeared more prosperous through the southern lens, the prosperity it saw wasn't for everyone. Fassino left Italy in 1886 and, by way of New York, found his way to an older brother working the coal-mining communities of Braidwood and Norris, Illinois. Giovanni joined the family to work the mines and save money for their own further opportunity. After their older brother returned to Italy, Giusseppi and Giovanni turned to farming, but it didn't take. So they changed their names to Joe and John, pooled their savings and moved to the Indian Territory, where they'd heard about an Italian settlement where they might find success selling imported foods to their countrymen.

The Fassinos struggled at first but refused to give up. They were known to smuggle products like imported cheese, chestnuts and figs into company camps where miners were forced to buy from a company store. Joe and John had to talk their way into guarded camps with goods hidden out of sight in their buggy.

Various strikes created the need for the Fassinos to extend credit to striking miners, which turned the store into a de facto bank for Italians. Italians at the time were often paid in script, and what money they acquired was more likely to be buried than kept in American banks.

"They say if you started digging around back in those days, you might've found something like $50,000 out there," said Steve DeFrange, curator of the Krebs Heritage Museum.

Joe Fassino kept track of savings and the wills of his depositors in case they died. Fassino saw opportunity to expand the services he extended, soon helping conduct business affairs and correspondence for his patrons, which eventually led to being named Italian consular agent about 1900. The position allowed him to perform a number of services for his countrymen, including currency exchange. It also allowed him to control the always-lucrative communication business, sending and receiving transmissions to and from Italy.

In 1897, the Fassino brothers established a macaroni factory in McAlester that reached markets in Arkansas, Kansas, Missouri and Texas, as well as a surplus sales region in the Caribbean. By the time Pete's Place opened in 1925, the Fassinos were pillars of the community where they owned large acreages and numerous business ventures. When Joe Fassino died in 1936, he was called the "Dean of Italians" in Pittsburg County.[22] Joe Prichard said he has little doubt his grandfather was using pasta products from the Fassino brothers at Pete's Place.

The Fassino brothers laid the groundwork for markets like Lovera's and Antonelli's years later. The one thing you won't find in Pittsburg County today that was prevalent in the old days is locally baked bread. Sam Lovera said the bread in Krebs in those days was terrific, dating back to the Shipley Baking Company installment in Bache, Oklahoma, just east of McAlester in Pittsburg County. Joe Prichard remembers that bread, too.

"My grandfather's sister, Rose Shipley," Joe said. "Their family had a bakery, a really big one. It was a multistate deal."

Before the Shipleys came to Bache to install an extension of their Fort Smith, Arkansas–based company, which had bakeries in Muskogee and Fayetteville, the bakery in Bache was opened by Louis Ferando in the early 1920s.

"It had a house built around this earthen oven. They built this oven into the side of a hill and basically built a house on top of it. You could smell it here [at Pete's Place] when it was going."

Prichard said they'd have extended family dinners there, with the Piegaris from Hartshorne coming up.

When the Shipleys' bakery closed, the mantel of the area's top baker went to Paul Antonelli, who had already established himself as an expert baker at Antonelli's Bakery & Grocery. Antonelli's eventually became the preeminent local bread supplier, whose clients included the five Italian restaurants that put Pittsburg County on the map. Antonelli's bread came from a one-hundred-year-old recipe created by Paul Antonelli, an immigrant from Lombardy, Italy, who arrived in the Indian Territory in the 1880s to trade with his *paisans* and their families who depended on coal-mining to make a living. Back in the Old Country, Antonelli baked classic oval-shaped bread in a handmade brick oven for his village. Antonelli opened his first bakery in Pittsburg County in Alderson, just a few miles east of Krebs. He would eventually take over the Bache factory in McAlester, and as his family grew and matured, the business expanded to Krebs. Paul was known for delivering via

22. Brown, *The Italians in Oklahoma*, 38.

horse and wagon in the old days, handing out tokens that read, "Good for 5¢, loaf of bread, Paul Antonelli Grocery & Bakery, LT."[23]

Karen Scarpitti said that her lifelong search for bread as good as the loaves made in Bache ended last year.

"I was in Venice last summer, they had three rooms of breakfast and one room was all bread. I told my daughter, 'You've got to come here. I've found bread that's so much like Bache bread!' My daughter looked at me, and she goes, 'What is Bache bread?'"

Rather than explain, Karen just made her daughter take a bite.

"We ate the whole freaking thing."

Paul Antonelli's bread recipe served Pittsburg County through three generations over ninety-seven years via his son Jim and grandson Paul Cortassa Sr.

"Paul Cortassa's uncle was named Jim Antonelli, who was a great baker," Sam Lovera explained. "Paul learned to bake from Jim, who had learned from his father. And when Paul got older, Paul put in a bakery and bait shop east of Krebs."

Cortassa delivered hard-crust Italian bread each morning about nine o'clock to Lovera's.

"It was still hot when it arrived," Sam said. "And he would deliver to the restaurants in the afternoon. He was selling nine hundred, one thousand loaves of bread a week, easy."

Cortassa raised four kids, each of whom earned college degrees and pursued new professions. So Cortassa sold the bait shop and grocery store to Benny Snell, who would eventually become mayor of Krebs.

"Benny was fine for a while because he had Paul's baker, Ed Wright," Sam explained. "When Ed turned sixty-five, he started drawing Social Security and Benny started trying to make the bread."

But Benny was neither a baker nor did he aspire to be one.

"You've gotta be passionate to be a baker," Sam said. "You've got to get up at 3:00 a.m. to let the dough rise; you're working day and night."

James Johns, who grew up two miles east of Krebs and only minutes from the bakery, remembers Benny Snell fondly, saying he misses the fresh doughnuts he used to serve each morning with a joke or clever comment. Johns, who now lives in Oklahoma City, said he'd rather have eaten a doughnut from Benny Snell than eat at any of the restaurants still standing in Pittsburg County.

---

23. Nancy Woodward, "Ethnic Loaves," *Oklahoma Today* 47, no. 1:111.

Chapter 7

LITTLE DIXIE PLAYGROUND

With as much bad fortune as the people of Pittsburg County have had to endure, between a wildly fluctuating economy and the many deaths incurred in the mines, it has also had some extraordinarily good fortune when it comes to advocacy.

Some of the most powerful men in the history of Oklahoma politics hailed from Pittsburg County, which brought to town not only the munitions plant but also Boeing and Lockheed to supply them. And those powerful politicians had a good friend over in Krebs.

Pete Prichard's marriage to Pasqualina didn't last. His second wife was Mary Scarpin, who bore him a son they named Billy Joe, perhaps a further act of assimilation from the by-now true-blue Pete Prichard. Billy Joe grew up working in Pete's Place, which, by the time he was grown, had developed a strong reputation for its food and Choc. He shared a lot of his father's qualities, including a passion and talent for being a man of the people. Billy Joe, however, recognized that those qualities would work just as effectively in a field other than the restaurant business: politics. Running as Bill Prichard, he was elected mayor of Krebs in the mid-1950s.

The youngest of Pete's children spent his entire life working at Pete's Place, but in that time, politics became a passion. In reflection, his son Joe says his father had practical reasons for pursuing an office that would be beneficial to the local restaurants, but Bill also used politics, whether by design or not, to help expand the restaurant's reputation beyond the borders of Pittsburg County and Oklahoma.

Mary Prichard. *Courtesy of the Prichard family.*

Pete Prichard turned the operation over to Bill in 1964, which forced Bill to put his political career on hold. But the political careers of three Oklahomans and a major league baseball star helped turn Pete's Place into a phenomenon.

After Pete Prichard put his son Bill in charge, he continued to roll raviolis by hand every day until his health wouldn't let him. He still made his way into the basement to tend a crock of Choc, but more and more it was Bill who was the life of the party in the dining room, while the folks in the dining room tended to be prominent local figures. One in particular would soon become one of the most powerful politicians in the United States.

"He was really good friends with Carl Albert," said Kathy Prichard, who grew up in Krebs and was a part of the minority in that she was neither Italian nor Catholic.

As fate would have it, the "Little Giant of Little Dixie" was born in McAlester five years after Pete Prichard arrived to join his father in Krebs. Albert was raised in Bugtussle, just north of McAlester, by a coal miner/ farmer in a log cabin. Albert went west to the University of Oklahoma in 1927, graduating Phi Beta Kappa in 1931, and then studied at the University

Carl Albert, the former Speaker of the United States House of Representative, outside his home in McAlester. *Photo used with permission from the* Oklahoman.

of Oxford as a Rhodes scholar. Albert was elected to Congress for the first time in 1946 and appointed House Majority Whip in 1955, eventually rising to House Majority Leader in 1961. In all, Albert represented southeastern Oklahoma for thirty years. Albert served as Speaker of the United States House of Representatives from 1971 to 1977. No Oklahoman has ever held a higher political office. He was also a frequent diner at the Krebs restaurants and quick to bring his high-powered friends from the nation's capital for lamb fries, Italian food and Choc beer.

"Carl Albert brought a lot of political figures and dignitaries to Pete's Place," Kathy said.

Karen Scarpitti recalls Carl Albert eating at Minnie's as a child, but she said her favorite dignitary wasn't from Krebs.

"I loved when Mrs. Kerr came in," Scarpitti said of former Oklahoma governor Robert S. Kerr and his wife. "I just thought she was so elegant, and she smelled so good!"

But Carl Albert wasn't the only famous person showing off Oklahoma's Little Italy to his celebrity friends. Hall of Fame pitcher Warren Spahn was born in Buffalo, New York, on April 23, 1921, but through much of his baseball career, the family's primary home was the Diamond Star

Celebrities like David Rubenstein were commonly seen at Pete's Place with owner Pete Prichard. *Courtesy of the Prichard family.*

Ranch south of Hartshorne in Pittsburg County. "Spahnie," who won 363 games in his long, illustrious career, and his family spent winters in Pittsburg County. The Diamond Star Ranch was a paradise for hunting and fishing, and the winningest left-handed pitcher in major league history was glad to host major leaguers who loved the outdoors as much as he did. The walls at Pete's Place are littered with photographs of major league ballplayers. After long days hunting in the ample hill country of Pittsburg County, these same players unwound with steaks, pasta, lamb fries and lots of Choc.

"I remember Billy Martin coming in here," Joe Prichard said. "What a deal that was."

Spahnie wasn't the only baseball star who haunted the spaghetti-and-lamb-fries circuit. Dominic Silva Jr. remembers Pepper Martin being a regular at his grandmother's restaurant, Minnie's Italian Dinners. The former Gashouse Ganger known as the Wild Horse of the Osage,

Pete Prichard with the Singing Cowboy, Monte Hale, one of his many celebrity diners. *Courtesy of the Prichard family.*

Martin eventually became the athletic director at the Oklahoma State Penitentiary.[24]

Big-name national figures helped build the reputation for Pete's Place and all of Pittsburg County, and two of the county's most prominent sons helped bolster that reputation from the state capitol. Gene Stipe was born in Blanco, south of McAlester, in 1926 to Jacob and Eva Lou Stipe, who owned a farm up on Peaceable Mountain, just south of McAlester but now within the city limits. When Jacob couldn't makes ends meet via farming, which was often, he turned to the coal mines for income. Stipe grew up in poverty, and part of his legacy in fifty-three years on the Oklahoma State legislature is his championship of the poor and deprived. But Stipe's legacy is more frequently remembered for his brushes with the law. His long career, which included helping Carl Albert establish the state's vocational-technical

24. Associated Press, "Pepper Martin In Prison Job," *Lawrence Journal-World*, October 6, 1960.

system, is most remembered for dodging indictments until he finally couldn't dodge them anymore. Stipe began his service to the Oklahoma House of Representatives at the age of twenty-one in 1948. The former navy man served as assistant floor leader from 1949 to 1953 and earned his law degree from the University of Oklahoma while serving in the state House of Representatives and living at the fire station in Norman, Oklahoma. Stipe had one two-year break from his legislative career when he ran for a senate seat against then-incumbent Kirksey Nix and lost in 1954. Nix—whose son Kirksey Nix Jr. would rise to a leadership role in the infamous Dixie Mafia, is currently imprisoned for the murder of a New Orleans grocery executive and was suspected of attempting to assassinate Sherriff Buford T. Pusser in Tennessee—left for the Oklahoma Court of Criminal Appeals in 1956. Stipe won Nix's seat in a special election that year and didn't give it up until 2003, when he confessed to making illegal campaign contributions.

Regardless of his tarnished record of service to Oklahoma, Stipe was doggedly protective of Pittsburg County and was quick to bring visitors to Krebs to share the local fare and a handshake with his good friend Billy Joe Prichard.

Liz Prichard, one of Frank's children who now helps operate Roseanna's, said, "I remember going to Grandpa's [Pete's Place] and seeing Senator Stipe eating back in the kitchen, where he [Pete Prichard] kept a table."

While Stipe might've held state office longer than anyone ever has in Oklahoma, he didn't rise to the state's highest office. George Nigh did. Born in McAlester a year after Stipe, George Nigh attended public schools in McAlester, where he was childhood friends with both Bill Prichard and Dom Giacomo. Nigh taught at McAlester High School from 1952 to 1958, but his teaching career came to an end in 1958 when he was appointed to become the state's youngest lieutenant governor. In 1963, Nigh became the seventeenth governor of Oklahoma, filling an unexpired nine-day term following the resignation of Governor J. Howard Edmondson. Nigh was elected lieutenant governor for three consecutive terms in 1966, 1970 and 1974 before he was elected governor in 1978. He also became the twenty-second governor of Oklahoma, serving five days to fill an unexpired term following the resignation of Governor David Boren before taking over his regular term and winning reelection in 1982. His campaign manager in Pittsburg County was Bill Prichard.

"When I became governor, I told the folks back home not to name anything after me," Nigh recalled. "At least not while I was in office.

"Well, one day I get a call from Bill Prichard, who tells me I need to come home for a dedication of a new bridge they were naming after me. I told

Bill, 'I told you not to name anything after me,' and he just stayed after me to come home for this ceremony.

"So, I finally tell him I'll be there, and when I get to Krebs find out its a little wooden bridge on a new walking trail!"

Thanks to Bill's relationship with the state's highest-ranking officials, Pete's Place became a regular stop for politicians and campaigns through the decades. In June 1991, both Stipe and Nigh joined a luncheon at Pete's Place as part of the Oklahoma City Chamber of Commerce's Goodwill Tour. During the event, the mayor of McAlester waxed and joked about Pittsburg County's favorite sons: Carl Albert, George Nigh and Gene Stipe. When Nigh took the podium and was in the midst of his rejoinder to the mayor, a thunderclap shook the foundation and shook the dishes. Nigh turned to the mayor and proclaimed, "I told you you shouldn't talk about Gene Stipe like that!"

With the endorsement of both local and national dignitaries, Pete's Place and Minnie's Italian Dinners had created enough interest in the cuisine of Pittsburg County for a third major restaurant to open.

Chapter 8

ISLE STYLE

Dominic Anthony Giacomo (sometimes pronounced JACK-omo, other times simply Gee-A-Como) was a man of such profound vision that it took something spectacular to take his eyes off the prize. Taking a break, probably with a cigarette, from his duties in the galley aboard a navy ship sailing through the Tyrrhenian Sea off the Sorrentine Peninsula on the south side of the Gulf of Naples, Dom's eye was caught. The young sailor from Krebs serving his country during World War II stared long toward the shore of the Campania region of Italy, homeland to so many from his own humble home in southeastern Oklahoma. His grandparents had come from Italy in 1895, though a little farther north in Castiglione. Suddenly, the vision before him fused with the vision in his mind. Dom grew up working in Pittsburg County restaurants like the Pig 'n' Whistle and Pete's Place, learning the system and hustling up money for the family. The work was hard, but the connection with people and the possibilities a restaurant promised for a dreamer like Dom were intoxicating. Rare was a minute working in those restaurants when he wasn't planning for his own place. Dom came from a family and a community that knew how to cook authentic, old world Italian food, but Dom was born to sell the sizzle.

Off the coast of the Isle of Capri, Dom Giacomo's vision for a restaurant in Krebs began to come together. He didn't have a building, real estate or the money to buy either one, but he had a name to call the restaurant he was determined to build as a tribute to his mother: the Isle of Capri.

Spaghetti is at the center of what makes thousands of people show up in Pittsburg County every week for lunch and dinner.

"Dom was a great guy," said Sam Lovera. "I loved that guy. He was just amazing. He had big ideas and balls of steel. He wasn't afraid of anyone or anything. He just went for it."

And when Dom Giacomo returned to Krebs after the war, he did go for it. He went back to Pete's Place to work and continue to learn from Pete Prichard, who was an uncle to Dom through his first marriage.

"Pete and Dom were really close," Lovera said. "They were a lot alike, personality-wise, and they just got along great."

So great that Lovera said Dom would be entrusted to run Pete's Place when the Prichards went on vacation."

"Pete was a great guy, and everybody loved him, but he wasn't a businessman," Lovera said. "He was very generous and was always giving people free food and stuff like that. He had some customers who would come in and Pete would comp them appetizers and stuff that they would fill up on and then not order any entrees. Well, Pete goes on vacation to California and leaves Dom in charge. When those folks came in, Dom wouldn't comp 'em anything. So when Pete got back, the people were complaining about Dom, but that's just the way he was. He didn't see any reason for these people to get a free ride. And he was right!"

Dom continued to play a prominent role at Pete's Place while saving what he could to fulfill his dream. As much vision as Dom had, he had just as little patience. So, when an old prisoner-of-war camp was flagged for demolition, Dom pounced on the opportunity and laid claim to the lumber. Meanwhile, he had a plot of property picked out just east of Pete's Place. There was only one problem.

"Dom started building the Isle of Capri on property he didn't even own," Dominica Lovera said. "He just started building; he didn't care. He was just determined, and he wasn't going to let anyone stop him."

And he didn't. The property owners sold the land to Dom, draining what savings he had plus money acquired through the GI Bill, so when the Isle of Capri opened on Mother's Day in 1950, it had to work.

Young Dom Giacomo, who grew up much of his life without a father, would eventually open Isle of Capri as a tribute to the mother who raised him and his five siblings through the Great Depression by selling Choc beer and Italian food out of their home. *Courtesy of the Giacomo family.*

"He built it on the order of a house, so if it didn't work out, he and his mother would live there," said his nephew by marriage Don Robertson in an 2000 interview in Oklahoma City's the *Oklahoman*. "It started out with one dining room."

Dom Giacomo was one of six children born to Jim and Rose Giacomo. Jim came to Krebs in 1903, leaving behind his wife, the former Rose Choch. Jim settled in a shanty encampment called Boxtown, where he found enough work in the mines to save up for a home in Krebs and send for Rose, who bore him six children. Jim found work enough to provide for his family but died in 1934. Rose's sister Pasqualina had been married to Pete Prichard. The sisters played key roles in the success of Pete's Place, and Rose was best friends with Minnie Peccio, who had survived hard times with her restaurant. Rose followed her

Minnie Peccio raised three children while running a restaurant as a single mother. *Courtesy of the Peccio family.*

This is the oven built by Jim Giacomo for his wife, Rose. *Courtesy of the Giacomo family.*

lead, using the brick oven Jim had built for her to bake bread and the crocks prevalent all around Pittsburg County to make Choc beer.

Dom grew up in awe of his mother, who used the oven to dish out pizza and sold homemade Italian sausage, ravioli and her own version of caciocavallo cheese. Rose was the embodiment of determination and an inspiration to young Dom. Rose fought to make ends meet, and Dom recognized it. He knew how little the family had and how little Rose had to trade and was inspired to ensure that her hard work didn't go unrewarded. Dom was also a dreamer, so when he washed dishes at Pete's Place or the Pig 'n' Whistle it was partially to help the family but mostly to learn and build toward his dream.

"Uncle Dom always talked about how he would have his own place some day and give his mama her due," Rose Ann Robertson said.

Before joining the navy and that fateful trip around the Isle of Capri, Dom opened a place in McAlester called the Plantation Club.

"That was his first little adventure in restaurants," said Robertson, who—along with her husband, granddaughter and any other kin who might be in town on a given day or night—operates the Isle of Capri today. But make no mistake: despite all the extra hands, Rose Ann has the last word. And her last word never strays from Uncle Dom's shadow.

"Uncle Dom did everything *his* way," she said. "And his way was right, so that's how we do things today."

The neon sign out front of the Isle of Capri today is the same one that's burned since day one. The only thing that's changed is the size of the restaurant.

The sign that stands out front of the Isle of Capri today is the same one that was there when it opened back in 1950.

"I did an expansion on the place back in the late 1990s that quadrupled the size of the place," Rose Ann said. "But I tried to keep things the way I thought he'd want it."

The way Dom wanted things in 1950 was first about the family. His family has always cooked, cleaned and waited tables at the Isle of Capri. And they've always served a standard, family-style Krebs menu, thanks to what Dom had learned in his time at Pete's Place: steak, fried chicken, lamb fries and the Italian food on which his mother built her own sterling reputation. The money, though, was in Choc beer and the table wine they served—illegally.

"We were raised on Choc beer. My uncle would have these little-bitty mugs, and he'd call us over, and say, 'Go on, get you a little drink of Choc beer,' we were just little-bitty things. And you know what? None of us drinks. None of us is interested in drinking."

Because Choc beer was illegal, it was pure profit, which helped Dom build up a savings to improve the Isle, purchase property and dream even bigger. Perhaps his biggest dream come true was, of all things, a gas station he built next door to GiaComo's in 1965.

"That gas station was something else," Rose Anne recalled. "You just can't imagine how people were in awe of it. It was so futuristic."

Dom Giacomo's crowning achievement might've been his GiaComo's Texaco, promoted as "the world's most space-aged service station." *Courtesy of the Giacomo family.*

Sam Lovera recalled the station, which was once advertised as "Giacomo's Texaco, the World's Most Beautiful Space Age Service Station."

"It was like something from *The Jetson's* or something," Sam said. "It was spectacular, but that's how Dom did things. He was just a really inspiring guy."

After the navy outpost was built in the 1940s, the old Texas Road that helped establish McAlester became a part of the new U.S. Highway 69. Dom recognized the opportunity and built a sparkling new restaurant on the highway. This one, which he would call GiaComo's, was sleek and modern, continuing with the Frank Lloyd Wright–style architecture, but this one was spectacular for its time. The interior included a fountain in the lobby, a ceiling that changes color and walls covered either in painted mirrors or plastered rock. And not much has changed.

"Everything is original," Dom's nephew Wendell Brewer said.

The only real change over the years has been to add an extra dining room on the north side of the restaurant, but otherwise, Dom's vision in 1959 remains intact. Next door, he built a service station, which exceeded the style of GiaComo's. Its streetlights looked like postmodern angels prepared to take flight, and the roof over the station followed a similar concave design. Under that roof was a two-story enclosure with a twisting stairway encased in glass and stacked-rock walls.

"That place was amazing," Sam Lovera recalled. "It was just like Dom. It was so ahead of its time. You should've seen that place. He really was a genius. Way ahead of his time."

Dom's niece concurred, saying, "It was beautiful, but that was Uncle Dom. He had real style."

GiaComo's was run by Dom's brother Nick. Like his brother, Nick Giacomo started working early in life. Born in 1913, Nick became a lamplighter at age nine. Each night he'd ride on horseback around Krebs, lighting street lamps, and then he would go by the same lamps in the morning to snuff them out. Nick did that until he turned twelve, when he started joining his father in the coal mines. He married Eolia Duff in 1935, and together they raised two daughters, Delores and Dora Lea. Before his brother got him into the restaurant business, Nick worked in the Civilian Conservation Corps and at the Naval Ammunition Depot before taking a job delivering Grapette and Dr Pepper in the late 1940s that helped him in the days ahead as restaurant operator.

"People knew him all over," Wendell Brewer said. "I don't care where we were, people everywhere knew him, Atoka, Durant, Denison, anywhere, and everybody knew him.

Above: A postcard featuring an aerial view of GiaComo's shortly after it was built in 1959.

Right: Wendell Brewer and his niece Heather Solomon work at GiaComo's, which was run for years by Nick and Eolia Giacomo.

Today GiaComo's is run by Nick's daughter Dora Lea and her son Wendell Brewer with help from Heather Solomon, Nick's great-granddaughter. Wendell said he's been working in GiaComo's since he was a child.

"I waited my first table when I was ten years old, I'll never forget it," he said. "Dom wasn't in here too much, but he'd come by and everybody knew it when he was here. I was scared to death of that man. He had that flattop hair cut, *big* guy. He look over at me and said in that *deep* voice of his, 'Get over there, and get an order off that table.' Like I said, I was scared to death of him, so I run over and get me a pencil and pad, only ten years old, and took their order."

The menu at GiaComo's is similar to its cousins in Krebs: steak, chicken, lamb fries, meatballs ravioli and lasagna. Wendell said the top two sellers are steak and lamb fries.

"We're known for our steaks," he said. "Every year we win the award for best steaks in town."

Wendell said back in 1989 or '90, he added sauté-pan items, which none of the other restaurants did at the time. GiaComo's was also first to offer shrimp scampi. Heather, Wendell and Dora Lea also offer classic chateaubriand, chicken Florentine, veal Parmigiana and Alfredo with shrimp or a seafood mixture.

With business still on the rise after two decades, Dom doubled the size of the Isle of Capri in 1970. A fire in 1972 stalled things for a bit, but not for long. Dom was a force of nature who played by his own rules.

"I remember there was this time when Dom owed my dad a little money, and he'd still come in to get product for the restaurant like it was no big deal. My dad would say, 'Dom, when are you gonna pay me that money?' and Dom would slap the counter and laugh that huge laugh of his and say something like, 'Oh, Mike, you're funny…you know I'll pay you back,' and so forth.

"Well, a piece of property came available that my dad knew Dom wanted, so my dad went over there and put the earnest money down on it," Lovera said. "Sure enough, Dom comes in about a week later and says, 'Mike, I see you put earnest money down on that corner lot.'"

Dom then offered to pay Mike a portion of what he owed him to walk away from the deal, but Mike refused.

"So, you know what Dom did?" Lovera said. "He left and waited for my dad to go run an errand, and he came back and offered to pay the money he owed to my mother and asked her to talk to my dad for him about letting that lot go."

Sam Lovera laughs when he tells the story today, but his kinship and respect for Dom Giacomo is impossible to miss.

"He was just such an interesting guy," Lovera said. "Probably one of the most interesting people I've ever met. He just didn't care what anybody thought about the way he did things. I loved that guy.

"He used to come in the store to visit with my dad, and he had this big dog that rode around in the car with him. In the summer, he'd toss me the keys to his car and say, 'Sammy, take the car for a spin around the block to cool off my dog.'"

Dom's way of doing things set the Isle of Capri apart from Pete's Place, which, especially in the late 1960s and early 1970s, had slowed down following the passing of its patriarch, Pete Prichard. The "new" place, in some eyes, had surpassed Pete's Place.

"When I was in high school, we kind of looked at the Isle of Capri as the 'nice' one," said Kathy Prichard, who grew up in Krebs among the minority of folks with no Italian blood flowing through her veins. "We never ate out much in my house, but I did have two prom dinners at the Isle of Capri. I never set foot in Pete's Place until I started dating Joe."

"Billy Joe used to spend more time in the Isle of Capri than he did in Pete's Place," Roseanne Robertson said. "He and Dom were really close friends."

With two restaurants well established and his family helping run them both, Dominic Giacomo died in 1974 of a heart attack at age forty-nine. Joe Prichard from Pete's Place remembers him fondly.

"We always called him Uncle Dom," Joe said. "He was just a bigger-than-life character. A true original."

The family was devastated, but they loved Dom so much and appreciated how much he'd put into the business, so they rallied around his sister Minnie Duff to keep the restaurant serving the food that had made it famous.

"We have not varied in our cooking in the forty years since I've been working there," Robertson said back in 2000.[25] "We've kept the style just the same. That was our uncle's wish."

More than a dozen years later, that hasn't changed. Dom's great-niece Stephanie Fields handles daily operation of the restaurant with her aunt by marriage Julie Duff. Both of them cook, wait tables, mix drinks, wash dishes, vacuum, arrange caterings or private parties, answer the phone, clean the bathrooms and mix with the locals—just as Uncle Dom would've done.

The Isle of Capri is a large white house that looks a little like an old-school supper club. Next door is a home clearly inspired by the architecture of Frank Lloyd Wright. A curved concrete pathway connect the house to the parking lot of the Isle of Capri. This is where Dom lived. While the Isle must've looked like the hottest thing since the mambo in 1950, today it appears frozen in time. And that's part of the charm. While Pete's Place has undergone a lot more updating in recent years, the Isle of Capri is probably closer to its original vision. It's not a museum, but

---

25. Lori Yost Nelson, "Authentic Italian Tastes Cooking in Krebs," *Oklahoman*, December 10, 2000.

Left: Stephanie Fields (left) and Julie Duff are part of the long line of family who have contributed to the success of the Isle of Capri.

Middle: The home of Dom Giacomo is next door to the Isle of Capri.

Bottom: Dom Giacomo's home was inspired by the designs of Frank Lloyd Wright.

it might be a time machine. Interior walls are whitewashed and heavily mirrored. Strings of festive lights wind around a spiral staircase that leads to a private banquet room upstairs, which could easily be the secret lair of Austin Powers.

Beyond the standard Krebs fare, you can order the Isle Style white spaghetti, which is spaghetti pan-tossed with butter, olive oil and loads of garlic with a little house-made olive salad to give it a rich, piquant finish. The oven-roasted French fries are hand-cut and a local favorite. Desserts include variations on cannoli, Kentucky bourbon pie, tiramisu and spumoni.

Three dining rooms boast about 250 seats and could probably squeeze in 300 if the fire marshal was on vacation. There is nothing corporate or slick about the Isle. This is a family affair, with the quirky charm to prove it.

Both Fields and Duff tried out college and jobs they'd studied for—only to learn that the restaurant bug isn't an easy one to shake, especially when so many of your loved ones made sacrifices to keep it successful enough to sustain the family for generations.

"You grow up in it, and you get a hunger for it," Fields said. "It's like a production every night."

Duff continued, "You see the same people come in, and you know what they're going to eat, and what they're going to drink. And they've come to you because they love what you do."

"You become a part of special occasions, special moments in people's lives," Fields interjected. "I don't ever want to see this fail. This is our family heritage, and that means a lot to me."

Don Robertson said something in an article written years ago that is as true today as it was the day Dom first opened: "We emphasize the family. I think that's what has kept me in this business. I love my customers. They grow on you and especially if you can please them and give them a special night out. It does me great pleasure to see people leave satisfied."

Chapter 9

THE END OF AN ERA

B y the end of the 1960s, Pete's Place was a bona fide tourist attraction that drew celebrities from the worlds of politics, music and Hollywood. Bill was in charge, but Pete continued hand-rolling ravioli every day through the mid-1960s, until age and health wouldn't let him. While Pete's activities slowed down, his grandson Joe was growing fast and was fascinated with the family business at an early age. He loved to watch his grandfather work the kitchen, learning the Prichard way and collecting business data that led to his development and expansion of the family business from mom-and-pop stop to full-fledged roadside attraction.

"My grandfather loved that restaurant," Joe said. "Daddy loved the people as much as Granddad, but Granddad really loved to cook. My dad cooked, too, but not for long. He was the worst guy to be cooking next to you because you'd be doing your job with him next to you, and then look over and he'd be gone—and wouldn't come back. He'd be out their in the dining room entertaining folks, and that'd be it."

Pete Prichard died on May 1, 1970, leaving Bill to run things on his own. Bill did plenty to advance the fortunes of the business, though his time at the helm of Pete's Place wasn't as long as you might expect.

"My dad really only ran the restaurant by himself about fifteen years," Joe Prichard said. "I realize that's a long time in general restaurant terms, but it's not that long for an eighty-two-year-old restaurant."

Bill didn't change too much on his own, but change did find him. That change was indirectly related to one of Pittsburg County's most infamous landmarks, the Oklahoma State Penitentiary.

Pete and Bill Prichard work the stove at Pete's Place. *Courtesy of the Prichard family.*

Prior to 1908, Oklahoma sent its convicts to a penitentiary in Lansing, Kansas. The commissioner of Charities and Corrections at the time was a woman named Kate Barnard, who, in her time, received numerous complaints about the mistreatment of Oklahoma inmates in the Kansas Penitentiary. A tour of the Kansas correctional center in August 1908 inspired her to write a report recommending that all Oklahoma prisoners be transferred back to Oklahoma. Fifty inmates were placed on a train and moved to McAlester on October 14, 1908, to be housed in a former federal jail in McAlester. When another fifty inmates arrived, the hundred built their own stockade. In May 1909, construction began on the Oklahoma State Penitentiary using inmate labor. Some acreage was donated, and the state purchased about two thousand acres and helped relocate families with houses on the targeted property. In the end, the penitentiary would prove to help stabilize the local economy when coal fell out of favor, but it also had a direct connection with one of the darkest days in the history of Pete's Place.

Oklahoma's Pardon and Parole Board used to meet eight times a year at the state penitentiary to consider the fates of inmates eligible for early release. The assemblage typically would head for Pete's Place after clearing its docket. The visits of the Pardon and Parole Board to Pete's Place took on legendary status as an ever-growing group of officials, staff and friends would take up the bulk of the small restaurant, filling most of its private dining rooms. Plenty of steak, chicken and pasta were served, but the amount of Choc beer that flowed is what kept the party returning. Pete's Place was more than fifty years old at the time and was already established as a playground for some of Oklahoma's most influential people. So word spread about its practice of serving Choc beer, but the Alcohol and Beverage Control Board had little sway over the situation.

Bill and Joe Prichard in the kitchen at Pete's Place. *Courtesy of the Prichard family.*

"I was told by people who would know that agents were told not to worry about what went on at Pete's Place," Joe Prichard said.

On top of this regularly scheduled hootenanny, in July 1981, the Oklahoma Dental Association hosted a luncheon at Pete's Place to celebrate the dedication of a state historical site at Oklahoma's first dentist's office in Savanna, which is in southeast Pittsburg County. Almost fifty folks crammed into Pete's Place on a hot afternoon, including Pete's

A fight ensues for the last bottle of beer after family service at Pete's Place. *Courtesy of the Prichard family.*

most influential and passionate patrons: Carl Albert, George Nigh and Gene Stipe. Albert was no longer Speaker of the House, but Nigh was governor at this time and Stipe was entrenched in the state senate. None of that was a problem, but a dentist from Miami, Oklahoma, named Bill Goodman was in attendance that day, and he wasn't afraid to answer questions for a reporter from the state's largest newspaper.

On August 17, 1981, Joe Prichard was in Stillwater, where he'd just begun his sophomore year at Oklahoma State University.

"I'm a newspaper guy," Joe said. "I was then, and I am now. I used to go up to the student union, get some coffee or breakfast and sit down and read the paper. So, that day I settled in and unfolded the *Daily Oklahoman*, and there it was."

It was a Monday, and the headline across the top of the front page, just below the banner, read, "'Gentlemen's Agreement' Keeps 'Choc' Beer Flowing" with a mug shot of Bill Prichard plugged beneath the headline, next to the Krebs dateline.

In the story, ABC board chairman Joan Blankenship hinted that the restaurant was protected by its influential clientele. An anonymous agent said, "Krebs is the best example of hypocrisy of the whole system. Some of these guys have been chomping at the bits to bust Krebs but [ABC board member Richard A.] Crisp says he's not about to get involved in that."

The story also included Goodman's account of the dentists' luncheon, where pitcher after pitcher of Choc beer was served.

The reporter asked Stipe if the claim was true, but Stipe was in his prime of avoiding trouble. He'd already been before the grand jury more than once.

"Of course, I wouldn't know about that," he told the *Daily Oklahoman*. "The rooms are private. There is no way you can know what's being served in those other rooms."

But a local elected official from Pittsburg County was also quoted in the story, "I don't know of a politician who hasn't drunk Choc beer over there." The same official said he regularly visited other restaurants in Krebs where the illegal beverage was openly served.

The story detailed an account of a mid-1960s visit from First Lady "Lady Bird" Johnson. Lady Bird brought with her an entourage from the Washington press corps. An eyewitness told of seeing a member of the Washington Press flashing a sign at then U.S. senator Mike Monroney that read, "Do they still serve Choc beer at Pete's?"

The story also detailed the Pardon and Parole Board's "ritual" at Pete's Place. It included a quote from the parole board chairman at the time, Charles Chesnut, who sarcastically said of his post-docket soirees, "We are the essence of sobriety and the acme of propriety."

Chesnut went on to to say that the ritual had gone on during the entirety of his twenty-seven years as a board member. He also refused to go into detail with the reporter but suggested he talk to one of his colleagues who was usually in attendance.

That colleague was Bob Drummond, who covered the Pardon and Parole Board. Drummond admitted he'd been invited to and attended the ritual at Pete's. Furthermore, he said, "When Charlie's (Chesnut) there, they bring pitchers of Choc."

When confronted with that account, Chesnut said he had never asked what the ingredients were before saying, "I'm going to plead the fifth—or perhaps I should say the quart—on this one. I don't want to snitch on my friends."

In the story, Bill Prichard admitted he bought most of his stock from a local "widow woman." He also gave the quote that determined the headline: "It's kind of a tradition around here. We've always had sort of a gentlemen's agreement."

Joe Prichard put the paper down and went to find a telephone to call home. No one was in trouble yet, but now the question was whether or not to continue to serve the most profitable thing on the menu. It wouldn't be long before a little more serendipity helped Bill Prichard decide what to do.

"Two agents from the ABC showed up and attempted to order beer with dinner," Joe said. "It just so happened that they were out of beer that night—because it was made in a very crude, very imperfect science, and they'd run out all the time."

The agents ordered Choc with dinner, but none was delivered.

"They left two dollar bills on the table as a tip and their business card from the ABC between them. So my dad got scared and quit."

Joe spent the remaining two years pursuing a degree from Oklahoma State in hotel and restaurant administration. Prichard was young but ambitious. He had big plans for Pete's Place.

"Our goal was to build Pete's Place up to a point where we could pay someone well enough to handle day-to-day management."

And Joe would get the opportunity to build that plan up almost immediately when he returned from Stillwater with his degree and his new bride, Kathy. Bill desperately missed politics, so when Joe got home, he wasted no time handing over the keys to Pete's Place. Soon, Bill Prichard was mayor of Krebs again, and little Joe was all grown up and beginning the second life of Pete's Place.

Chapter 10

CHOC GOES LEGAL

Joe Prichard was only a year out of college in 1984 when he took over the reins of the family business. In the nearly three decades since he's taken over, Pete's Place has added to its menu and undergone drastic upgrades and expansion. Joe's menu now includes seventeen dinner choice versus the four with which the restaurant started. Choc beer, which has zigzagged in and out of the boundaries of law over the years, is now brewed on the up and up by fourth-generation Zachary Prichard. The Krebs Brewing Company brews a variety of beers that change with the seasons and the whims of the brewmaster. It's served on tap at the brand-new Choc Room, which opened inside Pete's Place in April. Guests can belly up to the bar and sample various beers brewed just outside the window.

The brewmeister is Michael Lalli, whose family was established in Pittsburg County back during the coal boom. Michael's keen sense of the science of brewing is all aimed at flavor. Exact measuring, mashing, malting, fermenting, bottling and sanitation are useless if the beer is bad.

"My next-door neighbor was a home brewer when I was in my early 20s," Lalli said in a 2007 interview with the *Oklahoman*. "It was pretty intriguing to me, because the beer was flavored."

Lalli has been at Pete's Place since the year Joe Prichard took over, working at the restaurant through high school and college and spending several years as kitchen manager. When Oklahoma changed its brew-pub laws in 1992, Joe and Michael began making plans to build a brewery from which to finally sell Choc legally.

But it took the same kind of divine providence to turn Michael Lalli into a full-time Choc brewer as it did to make Pete Prichard a restaurateur—injury.

"Joe has a condo in Colorado, and we were out there in the mid-'90s skiing and doing market research because Colorado is a hotbed of craft breweries," Lalli said. "I broke my ankle snowboarding and was on crutches for six months. In the downtime, since I couldn't work at the restaurant, I spent that time putting the brewery together."

Lalli said his skills as a homebrewer weren't useless, but they couldn't begin to prepare him for full-scale industrial brewing.

"The scale is radically different," Lalli said. "What helped me learn was brewing the same beer over and over. The telephone is a lifeline, too. The craft brewing community is pretty small, and we made a lot of friends over the years."

The company has grown steadily since 1996 and is now an award-winning brewer of craft beers in several categories.

Zach Prichard is president of the company and is overseeing its expansion beyond not only Oklahoma's borders but around the world.

"Italy has been a good market for us," Joe Prichard said.

Joe Prichard said the goal is for steady growth. The brewery floor tells the tale of its expansion, with each addition marked by a slightly different shade of flooring. In the span of eighty years, the family has gone from illegally brewing beer next to a basement bathtub to taking delivery of three sixty-barrel brew tanks, each one big enough to hold 120 kegs of beer.

"New York City called us," Prichard said. "With craft beers, even the big guys are doing it, because the mainline brands are flat or down. Distributors are clamoring to sell different kinds of beer."

While Krebs Brewing Company was built on Choc beer, the Prichards aren't betting on it taking the world by storm, so they've diversified their offerings.

"We can't really even make Choc in the brewery the way it was made in homes," Zach Prichard said. The fourth-generation Prichard explained that true Choc has a specific profile because of the lack of proper equipment.

"The hops aren't even malted," he said. And that's a problem if the brewer is interested in consistency. Prichard said the chemical reactions brewmeisters pay attention to don't even exist in home Choc brews. The Prichards use the original ingredients, but they are brewed under much less volatile conditions.

The Prichards started with one Choc label, but Joe always saw it as a building block.

"Variety is more advantageous for us, but it's logistically more complicated," Joe said. "We want Choc beer to be our flagship beer, the one associated with Pete's Place."

While it might seem adding Choc labels breaks the bounds of tradition, the Prichards see opportunity for growth. Joe is an aggressive, passionate businessman, and Zach has enough discipline to have graduated from law school so there will be no resting on laurels on their watch. They aspire not just to draw people to Pittsburg County, but make it a brand.

"We're a destination," Joe Prichard said. "Right now, people come for the food and the romance of Pete's Place, but the way things are going, it might be that people are coming to visit the brewery and are surprised to find out there's a really old restaurant next to it. That would be just fine with me."

Growth is essential to the long-term survival of Pete's Place, which sounds a little insane when you're talking about a restaurant closer to one hundred years old than fifty. That's because, despite the success of Pete's Place, there is no business model for it.

"I've had banks try to apply standard models to what we do, and I try to warn them it can't be done," Joe said.

Joe Prichard said he serves about one hundred people a day during the week, but that might mean just a handful of people on Monday or Tuesday with a little spike on Wednesday or Thursday. But on weekends, they might serve anywhere from eight hundred to one thousand people or more during the summer months.

"If people are coming from a long way away, they're best advised to call us and make arrangements."

If Pete's Place is too full, visitors to Pittsburg County need not fear: the Isle of Capri, GiaComo's and Roseanna's are there. And each of those restaurants all have ties to Pete Prichard.

Prichard Legacy Expands

Frank Prichard was one of Pete's sons from his first marriage. Frank married Rose Ann Morgan, an only child herself, who bore him twelve children.

"My mother always wanted a big family," said her daughter Liz Prichard, who helps run Roseanna's as she has her entire life.

To support those kids, Frank worked for many years at the munitions plant just south of McAlester but often talked with his father about opening a takeout restaurant that served the foods their family had made famous. When Frank was unexpectedly laid off in 1975, he and his family made the dream become a reality, opening Roseanna's the same year. His daughter

Emily said her father didn't want to call it Frank's Place, so he gave the restaurant his wife's name in its Italian form.

The idea was a hit, and before the place turned three years old, five tables were added for dine-in. But Frank broke his leg in 1978, which was bad enough, but while in the hospital, it was determined he needed open-heart surgery. Roseanna's subsequently closed, to the dismay of the locals. Within the next year, the family decided to resuscitate Roseanna's, purchasing and refurbishing the old white house that Claude Kiple had built for his wife, Mabel, in 1930 on the east edge of Krebs. The new Roseanna's opened on January 30, 1980, and legend has it that the Kiples have continued to protect their home, which has now swelled to 130 seats, with an occasional bump in the night.

Roseanna's is the youngest of Pittsburg County's big four and did not adopt the family-style service that the other three follow. The food in the little white house on the eastern edge of town serves similar fare to its cousin restaurants, but it uses the recipes unique to Frank's clan. The pasta sauce is their father's recipe, and the specialty of the house is gnocchi, an Italian dumpling made with potato, flour and eggs. Ravioli comes standard or fried. Dinners include Michael Prichard's contribution: steak and peppers. Roseanna's also serves Italian standards like eggplant Parmesan, spicy meatballs, Italian chef salads drizzled with homemade vinaigrette and Italian sausages, plus the Krebs standards of fried chicken, steak and lamb fries. Roseanna's also serves fried shrimp and focaccia pizza.

After Frank's death in 1988, his children unified to keep their father's dream alive.

"I remember when my dad used to come out of the kitchen wearing his apron, and it would be covered in tomato sauce and how embarrassed I'd get," Liz said. "But now when I look back on it, I understand how important that was. People loved him because he paid attention to whether their food was cooked the way they expected."

Rose Ann died in 2008, but Paul, Peter, Liz, Claire and Vincent still work to keep the youngest and smallest of the Pittsburg County Italian restaurants charging into its fourth decade in business, serving the fare that Pete began back in 1925 and for which the town of Krebs has become widely known.

Whether you visit Pete's Place or Roseanna's, you can rest assured that you will be able to eat the same foods conceived by the restaurants' founders.

"You can add things," Joe Prichard said, "but you don't take anything away from the menu. I'll be hanged from the tree out front if I make any major changes."

Chapter 11

GOOD THINGS COME TO THOSE WHO WAIT

S am Lovera named his youngest son after an uncle neither of them ever met. The first Giovanni Lovera died at the age of five after a tragic fall while playing in the hills of southeastern Oklahoma. It was a fitting tribute, considering Sam was named after another uncle he never met due to the deadly nature of life in coal country. As many triumphs as the descendants of Battista Lovera have had, they've also had more than their fair share of tragedy. Resolve has been a common trait of Marta Lovera's children. When Sam talks to his son, Giovanni, about the future, he encourages him to put things in order.

"I try to tell him to live his life, don't worry about what anyone else is doing," Sam said. "There is an order to do things in. The time is right when it's right. Don't push it."

The right time for Battista and Marta to come to Oklahoma was also the right year for the state to gain statehood: 1907. They were young, and stories brought back to Italy from Italians who'd spent time in the small coal-mining community of Krebs piqued his entrepreneurial interests. Sam Lovera believes his grandparents were drawn to Krebs by something that has drawn men abroad as long as we've been recording history.

"They paid them in gold back in those days," Sam said. "An uncle in Italy introduced me to a ninety-year-old man who spent two or three years in Krebs, and he told me he brought back gold."

Battista quickly found work and wealth through his bottling company. But frontier life was tumultuous at best. Work came in spurts and disappeared to nothing in a snap. Families followed the work along the coal strip across county and state lines, which made it difficult for the vendors who planted roots in Krebs.

Mary was born in 1917, delivered at the family homestead by the Loveras' next-door neighbor, who happened to be a midwife. The neighbor, Helen Patterson, delivered two children that day: Mary and her twin brother, Giovanni. But Giovanni's life was brief, killed at the age of five when he lost his balance and fell off a tall box he'd climbed moments before.

A little brother came three years later and was named Matteo, but everyone called him Mike. Unlike Mary, Mike wouldn't start school until the family had moved to Chicago. Mike was only five, but he didn't like school at all. The Loveras lived in an apartment not terribly close to school, and one day during first recess, little Mike decided he'd had enough of school and made his way through the streets

From left: Battista Lovera, Simone "Sam" Lovera and Marta Lovera. *Courtesy of the Lovera family.*

Simone and Battista Lovera in the R&L Bottling Company in Krebs. *Courtesy of the Lovera family.*

From left: Giovanni Lovera, Mary Lovera and Matteo "Mike" Lovera. *Courtesy of the Lovera family.*

of Chicago until he got home. Neither Battista nor Marta were happy about it; they made it clear that school was important and marched him back.

Battista worked at International Harvester, which manufactured agricultural machinery and construction equipment. It was the brainchild of J.P. Morgan, who merged five competing manufacturers into one publicly held entity, a practice that paved the path to Morgan's sprawling wealth. When the Great Depression hit, jobs evaporated, and Battista determined it was time to go back to Krebs, where they still had a home and a few prospects, including in the coal mines.

Battista begrudgingly took work at the Wheatley Sample No. 4 Coal Mine, but he refused to allow his oldest son to join him in misery that is coal mining. However, Sam was persistent, and Battista couldn't do anything to slow his son's desire to spread his wings—not in good conscience, anyway. Battista recognized that his oldest son had the same kind of ambition that drove Battista to come to Krebs from Italy and eventually build and operate the R&L Bottling Company, which specialized in bottling soda pop. The bottling plant did earn him enough money to purchase a homestead. After closing the bottling plant, Battista uprooted the family and moved to Chicago to pursue an opportunity to work at the burgeoning International Harvester, renting the family homestead to make extra money on the side. While in Chicago, Battista got Sam a job at International Harvester, too, and they both made enough money to put some away until the Great Depression halted the gravy train. Sam saved enough money to purchase a brand-new Model A Ford, which his younger sister Mary recalled riding back from Chicago to Krebs in 1930. Not only did Battista lack the heart to tell his son "no," but times were also tough and the family needed all the help it could get to make ends meet. Upon returning, Battista moved his tenants out of the family homestead and dismantled the bottling plant to sell off the wood used to construct it.

"He just put the wood out in front of the house and sold it little by little until it was gone," said Sam Lovera, who was named after his deceased uncle.

Battista was in his fifties and desperate enough to take work in the mines, and he held Sam off for several months before ultimately relenting. Father and son went to the Wheatley Sample No. 4 mine together on the night shift in late October, not knowing that explosive gas had accumulated in the face of a crosscut and aircourse after the line curtain was removed as coal was hauled out. On October 27, 1930, a mining machine cut into the crosscut, releasing the gas over the controller, which ignited it. Coal dust carried the explosion over the entire mine, taking the lives of thirty men, including Battista and Simone "Sam" Lovera. The rescue operation was brief, but the recovery of bodies was slow and painstaking. There was never any hope of finding survivors, according to reports at the time.[26]

"My grandfather didn't want to work in the mines at all," said Sam Lovera. "He had owned a bottling plant in Krebs before and moved to Chicago to work at International Harvester, but the Great Depression shut them down, and the family had just moved back to Krebs."

When Marta Lovera returned from the dual funeral for her father and son to find nothing of the family hog other than a blood stain in the snow, her anger turned into resolve. Marta studied the spot and knew right away this had been the work of some of her fellow Italians because they'd left nothing of the hog to waste. A broken heart couldn't have clouded how devastating it was to lose that hog. Marta learned how to make sausage in the Old Country and would teach Mary and Mike the technique. They would teach their children. At the end of the day, life on the coal-mining frontier was a daily exercise in survival of the fittest. She had lost this round, but she wouldn't lose another. As Marta made the long, slow walk back through the snow to her heartbroken family at home, she found the strength to set aside her anguish and find the fitness to survive the winter ahead and the hard days that followed. Marta Lovera then did what the widows before her had done: she sold the sausage she'd learned to make growing up in northern Italy and brewed the beer that was all the rage around town called Choc.

"People don't realize how hard it was back in those days," Lovera said. "Mining was hard, hard labor and the families had no safety net."

When Battista and Sam were killed, Marta was left with some preferred shares of International Harvester stock, but it was tied up in nonfunctioning

---

26. Associated Press bulletin, October 28, 1930.

banks, the victim of the stock market crash. To survive, Marta not only brewed Choc but also made sausage and cheese to make sandwiches for coal miners. She intensified her gardening and sold vegetables to local grocers. She also read and wrote letters in Italian for the many widows in the community who could not read or write. After a few years, those preferred shares started paying off twenty-five dollars each quarter, which was no small amount during the Depression. Marta went to her dying day telling the story of how those shares carried her family through its hardest times.

And Sam Lovera is quick to recount these stories, told through his aunt Mary, from his office above Lovera's Italian Market, which is the same room where he and his brother Mikey grew up.

The building that housed the Lovera family from 1946 to the present was built in 1910 and has changed little in the ensuing years. When Sam

Lovera's is in the same 1910 building where the market opened in 1946.

and his brother took over the store in 1987, they added some red and green awnings to highlight their heritage and reorganized the market where they had worked throughout their youth. Today, Lovera's manufactures the same sausage that Marta Lovera made to save the family. Marta's triumph then is illustrated today by caciocavallo gourds hanging over a deli counter filled with sausage coils made from her recipe, which are sold all over the world.

Mike grew up and joined a group of friends who moved to Detroit to work in an axle factory. It was steady work among a lot of familiar faces, including Joe Finamore, whose parents, Carmine and Maria Finamore, played a key role in the founding of Krebs' food culture.

Carmine Finamore grew up as a shepherd boy in Bagnoli de Trigno in the Molise region of southern Italy. Aside from tending sheep, Carmine's father taught him the butchering trade. Carmine took to the craft quickly and also learned the art of bargaining with farmers for their animals. Around 1910, Carmine took work in a stable and station house for horse-drawn carriages. He earned about four lire a day and saved enough to set sail on the *Duca D'Aosta* for America in 1916. From Ellis Island, he tracked down some fellow Bagnoli de Trigno villagers working in a paper mill in Fairmont, West Virginia, and took a job there for a few months. It was in West Virginia that he received a succession of letters from an older sister living in Krebs, beckoning him out to the coal boomtown. Carmine finally relented, and it was in Krebs where he met and married his wife, Maria, in 1918. Carmine took work in the mines until an enormous slab of rock smashed through the ceiling he was trying to settle with wooden props and landed inches from him. Carmine walked out of the mines that day and never returned, telling his boss, "I no wanna come down there. You think I'm goin' go die down there?" That near-death experience compelled Carmine to return to his trade: butchering.[27]

At the suggestion of a friend, he bought a small wagon and began selling fresh meat to the miners in town. He found a woman who lived east of Krebs who owned a substantial herd of goats and started purchasing half a dozen at a time to butcher, dress and store in an icebox on his wagon, which he toured around the camps and homesteads, selling as he went. Business was brisk enough to invest in beef, pork and whatever his customers began to request. But Finamore's customers were primarily coal miners, who, in the middle of the 1920s, started to see work dry up as oil began to devalue coal. So Finamore took his family to Youngstown, Ohio, where he worked in a rubber factory and butchered at a local market in his spare time. Like so

27. Brown, *The Italians in Oklahoma*, 35.

many of his contemporaries, frugality was a priority, and he eventually saved enough money to buy land back in Krebs. He and a brother-in-law still living in Krebs bought more than three hundred acres of defaulted property via auction in 1929, triggering the Finamore family's return to Pittsburg County. Carmine survived the Depression on his homestead, raising and butchering cattle. He stored beef in an icehouse in McAlester and soon became a primary supplier to the Italian villagers and local grocers.

He and Maria had four sons and a daughter. His son Joe was born in 1922. When Joe Finamore ran into Mike Lovera at a lunchtime game of euchre in a train boxcar outside an axle plant in Detroit, neither could have known just how intertwined their fates would be. Both Lovera and Finamore would soon join the United States Navy, serve in the Pacific theater and marry women back in Krebs in 1952. Mike's son Sam, named after his fallen older brother, and Joe's daughter Dominica would marry decades later, and their mutual grandson by marriage now mongers cheese bearing the Lovera name that is sold all over the world.

As with so many young men in the early 1940s, December 5, 1941, was a call to arms for both young men, though a medical condition delayed Joe's deployment. Mike Lovera wasted no time enlisting in the United States Navy, and he headed to boot camp at the Naval Station Great Lakes in Chicago. From boot camp, Mike was sent to the South Pacific, where he served his time and sent money home to his mother to save on his behalf. He left Krebs a boy but returned as a man, ready to stake his claim.

Marta Lovera, meanwhile, had married widower Steve Testa, and together they owned and operated a grocery store. When Mike returned to collect his savings, his mother made him an offer he couldn't refuse: buy the store so she and her husband could retire. Mike purchased the business in 1946, calling it Mike's Grocery and Meat Market in a thirty-six-year-old building that had lodging where he and his wife, Madeleine, would raise a daughter, Mary, and two sons, Mikey and Sam.

The market was designed like any Italian market, mixing staples with cold cuts, fresh cheeses, pasta and bread baked daily. Even though the building hasn't changed since 1910, the store that opened in 1946 had less space then than it does now.

"The back part of the store was leased out to a poker game," Sam Lovera said. "It was an arrangement made by my step-grandfather, Steve Testa."

So what's now a very small store was practically a walk-up window in the early days, allowing the local seniors to spin yarns and take turns winning each other's money.

The culinary history of Pittsburg County is based on Old World southern Italian classics like spaghetti. *Courtesy of the Prichard family.*

Meatballs, like these from GiaComo's, have been served in Pittsburg County for decades.

Steak, like this one from Pete's Place, has long been a menu standard in Pittsburg County's Italian restaurants. *Courtesy of the Prichard family.*

Cacicocavallo gourds hang from rope slung over piping above the deli at Lovera's Market. *Photo used with permission from the* Oklahoman.

Opposite, bottom: Lovera's sells half a dozen varieties of sausage.

One thing that makes dining in Pittsburg County unique is the omnipresence of lamb fries.

Ravioli and spaghetti with meatballs is standard issue at the Isle of Capri, GiaComo's, Pete's Place and Roseanna's.

The most unique thing about Pittsburg County's culinary history is Choc beer. *Courtesy of the Prichard family.*

Opposite, bottom: Pete's Place makes racks and racks of ravioli in house each week. *Photo used with permission from the* Oklahoman.

B.J. Howell, Michael Lalli and Joe Prichard show off varieties of beer made by the Krebs Brewing Company. *Courtesy of the Prichard family.*

The lobby and inner dining room at GiaComo's is under a ceiling with ever-changing colored lights.

The white "Isle Style" spaghetti is sautéed in garlic, olive oil and butter and mixed with house-made olive salad.

A cannoli from the Isle of Capri.

At the Isle of Capri, diners can enjoy lasagna, manicotti, spaghetti, lamb fries and cannoli.

Lasagna (front) and manicotti are newer entries to the menu at the Isle of Capri.

Shelves at Lovera's are populated with house brands and Italian imports.

The selection of house-made sausages at Lovera's ranges from classic Italian to kielbasa and chorizo.

Sam Lovera in his grocery store, which first opened in 1946 in Krebs. *Photo used with permission from the* Oklahoman.

The sausage case at Lovera's.

Roseanna's specialty is gnocchi.

Lasagna from Roseanna's.

Shrimp fettucini Alfredo from GiaComo's.

Sam Lovera works a ball of caciocavallo-style cheese.

A gourd of Lovera's caciocavallo chills in an ice bath.

Sam Lovera forms caciocavallo cheese into a gourd shape.

Every week, a group gathers in the cheese room at Lovera's to make caciocavallo cheese.

Ashton Gabriella Muhs represents the fourth generation of family working in the restaurant business since her great-great-uncle Dom Giacomo started things back in 1950. *Photo used with permission from the* Oklahoman.

Michael Lalli, who was born and raised in Pittsburg County, is head brewmeister for the Krebs Brewing Company. *Courtesy of the Prichard family.*

Pete's Place has grown exponentially since its opening in 1925. *Courtesy of the Prichard family.*

Above: Meatballs and ravioli come standard with meals at Pete's Place. *Courtesy of the Prichard family.*

Left: Lovera's processes its sausage in a small factory adjacent to the grocery store. *Photo used with permission from the* Oklahoman.

In the earliest days of the market, Mike spent nearly as much time sitting on the porch watching the interurban come and go as he did selling meat. But that wouldn't last. For one thing, the Pittsburg County Railway Company's trolley service, which began operation in the late 1890s and eventually offered service out to Hartshorne by late 1904, ceased operation in early 1947. But most importantly, it was the sausage that put Mike to work. Sam Lovera remembers "grinding out a hundred pounds of Italian sausage a day on average, using a little hand-stuffer to package it."

The Wagner sausage stuffer Mike purchased in 1955, which he and his boys used until 1985, now sits above the walk-in freezer. Legend has it the device stuffed more than one million Italian sausages before being retired.

Back in the mid-1980s, Mike Lovera said in an interview that he sold "900 to 1,000 pounds of sausage a week."[28] Sam grinds the sausage from pork shoulder just as his father did. But the back room Mike Lovera toiled in has been replaced by a small sausage factory adjacent to the market. Sam still uses the same northern Italian recipe and ingredients, and people still come from all over to buy his finished product.

Sam Lovera recalls that growing up above Mike's Grocery was never idle, and it was an early education.

"I loved it," Sam Lovera said. "We always had to work, but it taught us how to socialize with people."

Lovera said everyone pitched in at home, and no one ever questioned it because it was "just what we did."

"I tell my kids all the time, because they think they've got it so tough, it's always easier as time comes forward."

Lovera said that he and his brother would get up early to help his father's driver make early-morning deliveries. But when that driver died of a heart attack, thirteen-year-old Mikey and twelve-year-old Sammy were the only "hired" hands Mike Lovera had until the boys moved out of the house more than ten years later.

"We did all the deliveries," Sam said. "People would call in every day—especially on Saturdays, that was a big day—it was the same dozen or so people who were getting older and couldn't get out that would call in their orders every day, and we had morning deliveries and afternoon deliveries.

"We had an old station-wagon, and it would be full of groceries and also malt and hops," Sam explained. "And if the people weren't home, we'd just walk right in and put the refrigerated stuff in their refrigerator. We'd pick

---

28. Woodward, "Ethnic Loaves."

The Lovera boys (from left) Mikey, Mike and Sam. *Courtesy of the Lovera family.*

up soda pop bottles, get the deposits. You look back on it, and it was just ludicrous when you think about the way we live today."

Among the most popular goods they delivered were malt, barley and hops to the myriad of local Choc makers. Mikey and Sammy were often invited to enjoy a glass of the Choc for which the malt, barley and hops were necessary.

"We grew up drinking Choc or wine every day," he said. "We knew you weren't supposed to drink too much of it, [but] it wasn't any kind of a big deal at all."

Lovera credits his work ethic to those early days, though he admits the workload might've been a little more than was fair, but it's hard to argue with the result.

"We'd get off from school early, and come home and work," he said. "Sundays, the store was closed, but that was when we restocked shelves or took inventory."

The store was closed Sundays, though often only in theory, because two decades of business and plenty of weekend traffic had taken word of mouth all over the region.

"Seems like every Sunday we'd have somebody knocking on the door from out of town," Lovera said. "My dad would always, always, always let them in. He'd say, 'These people drove from an hour or more to come here, we can't just tell them to go away.'"

The family store was a success for many reasons beyond the sausage, not the least of which was its proximity to the interurban trolley stop, which allowed easy access for folks from McAlester, Dow, Hartshorne and Haileyville. Mike Lovera also cultivated a deep, rich friendship with Bill Prichard, who was not only mayor of Krebs in the late 1950s but also took over ownership of Pete's Place from his father in 1964.

"Bill Prichard was godfather to my brother, Mike," Sam said. "Bill was the guy who would take us to Cardinal games because he knew we liked to listen to the games on the radio."

Sam said those games were often a subject of consternation for his father, who was quick to remind the boys they didn't have time to stand around and listen to the radio.

"Bill was a great guy. He was always encouraging us to see the world and go after our dreams. He knew we love the Cardinals, so he'd say, 'Man, you wanna go to St. Louis? I'll take you.' He took us to minor league games in Tulsa all the time."

Billy Joe Prichard was also a frequent guest at the Loveras' breakfast table.

"Bill used to come over every Sunday for breakfast," Sam said. "We'd go to mass at seven, get home about eight or eight-thirty and make breakfast at nine, and Bill would come up."

Joe Prichard remembers those breakfasts, too.

"It was nothing fancy," Joe said. "Just eggs and sausage and some kind of bread or biscuits, but I remember how good it was."

After breakfast, Mike and the boys would go down into the market and get Bill's restaurant order ready and send it home with him.

The Loveras seldom ate out, but when they did, it was rarely anywhere other than Pete's Place.

"Three or four Sundays a year, my dad might say, 'Let's go over to Pete's Place,'" Sam Lovera said. "We almost never ate out. We would carry it out from Pete's Place sometimes, but Mama cooked almost every day of the year—I don't know how she did it."

All that repetition combined with easy access to quality ingredients turned Madeline Lovera into an excellent cook. So good, in fact, that when you walk into Lovera's Italian Market today, one of the most prominently displayed products is the Lovera's Famous Old World Style

Spaghetti Sauce, which features Madeline Lovera's picture in the center of the label.

What Sam and his older brother Mikey lacked in social opportunities was overshadowed by the education in commerce they got.

"We learned to save our money," Sam said. "Daddy paid us in cash, and we didn't have anything to spend money on. I probably had between $15,000 and $20,000 saved up when I was twenty-two."

Matteo "Mike" Lovera behind the counter at was once called Mike's Grocery and Meat Market but is now Lovera's. *Courtesy of the Lovera family.*

Sam admitted his Italian frugality played a role in his saving, but that penchant for gambling that ran through the streets of Krebs also buoyed their bank accounts.

"Me and Mikey were pretty good bookies," Sam said, trying hard not to grin. "We learned real quick you cannot make money betting…The house always wins."

College was never discussed for Mikey or Sam Lovera, even though it was a foregone conclusion that their sister Mary would get her degree. Sam said he never really thought much about college, but he did want to take Bill Prichard's advice and see the world, so at age twenty-two, Sam told his father he planned to take a trip to Europe. Young Lovera spent nine months bumming around Europe in the early 1970s, where he met inspiring young people from around the world with a view of life, love and the pursuit of happiness that interested him. He returned to the United States with a new sense of purpose and was smart enough to recognize his own acumen with numbers. Sam went to the University of California, where he earned a degree in economics. He returned to Krebs planning to spend a year saving money before moving to London. But that's when he reconnected with Joe Finamore's daughter Dominica, who had spent a good part of her youth cooking in restaurants and catering kitchens in Oklahoma City. She was back in Pittsburg County working in local hospitals, where her father spent his entire professional career as a lab technician. Sam and Dominica married in 1988 and have raised four children together. Sam stayed in Pittsburg County but had plans to move on when the right opportunity arose.

"In 1986 or so, I went down to Dallas. I wanted to open a store down there—probably would've been a good idea now looking back on it," Sam said. "I told my dad about it, and he just thought that was the craziest idea he'd ever heard."

The next year, a month before his sixty-eighth birthday, Matteo Andrew "Mike" Lovera died.

"My dad was a great guy. He helped a lot of people," Sam said. "You know, we had over two hundred credit accounts at one time.

"My dad woke everyday at 6:00 a.m., walked downstairs and worked till six-thirty or seven o'clock at night six days a week for thirty years. He never took a day off, never took a vacation. He was just a hardworking guy."

And now that he was gone, he needed his boys to keep the family business alive, and they did. Sam and Mikey returned home to lend support to their mother, but it quickly became evident that change was needed.

"My brother Mike and I came home to try to keep the thing going," Sam said. "First thing we did was tear down some buildings and put in a large warehouse where we make the sausage now. I had a degree in economics from the University of California, so everything I did was from a business perspective."

Sam recognized that the neighborhood grocery he grew up in was disappearing from the consumer landscape.

"When the big supermarkets started coming in back in the '70s, places like this started to disappear," he said. "We thought we could revive interest in a store like the one we grew up in if we changed the inventory to premium products, whether it was the sausage and cheese made here or with products imported from Italy."

Mikey even helped establish an Ethnic Festival to replace the Italian Festival that Krebs handed over to McAlester years ago. The Ethnic Festival was held in the fall on the grounds of St. Joseph's Catholic Church, and food choices included Italian sausage sandwiches and spaghetti dinners, Chinese egg rolls, Indian tacos, Polish sausage and barbecue. Dessert included pastries, Czechoslovakian *kolache* and Italian *pizelle* and cannolis. Indian, Mexican, Italian and Czechoslovakian neighbors danced, while children attended the carnival and watched puppet shows. The event didn't last through a change at St. Joseph's, but it served the purpose of keeping the legend of Krebs in the local consciousness, helping bridge Lovera's to a time when it would be able to create an international market for itself.

But first, Sam's economic perspective would be put to full use as a retail giant embarked an all-out assault on rural America.

"When Walmart came to town, I thought it was going to be the end for us," Sam said. "But it just motivated us to change."

And change they did. Soon, Mike's became Lovera's Italian Market. Sammy bought a convenience store just south of the market on Washington Street, which cuts through the center of town, and transferred all the general merchandise into it. The brothers then stocked their family market with imported olive oils, tapenades, cheeses, pastas, sweets and other antipastos and continued selling cheese created by a local woman named.

Sam says the secret of their success is upholding a tradition started by his father: never compromising on the quality of ingredients.

"We use fresh garlic in our sausage," Sam said. "People compromise on ingredients all the time, but then you end up with a product that tastes just like everybody else's."

Today Lovera's Italian Market is only part grocery store; it's at least half time machine. Walk through the door, and it's as if this 103-year-old building is wrapped in time-resistant tape, protecting its interior from technological advancement past the 1960s. In the 1960s, the building and the makeup of the store weren't all that unique. But the sausage was. Lovera's sausage comes from Marta's original recipe, brought to Krebs from the Piemonte region from which Battista and Marta hailed. It was unique even within the Italian community in Pittsburg County because most of its Italian immigrants came from the south, where fennel is a staple ingredient in home sausage.

"The sausage in northern Italy doesn't have fennel in it. The main ingredients are garlic and black pepper," Sam Lovera said.

There are other secrets Sam isn't about to divulge about the sausage that has been a staple of their business for more than half a century. Today, Lovera's offers a half dozen varieties of sausage. It's sold both raw and smoked.

Sam also added to his inventory.

"A lot of places scrimp on inventory," Sam said. "But I think you've gotta give people lots to choose from. I save money in different places so I can make sure to offer the best."

To do that, Sam goes on buying tours of Italy and Sicily pretty much every year. So when food became the next cool new thing in the era of e-commerce, Lovera's was well positioned to prosper.

But there is no substitute for a trip to Krebs. Swing the front door open, and you'll swear what you see should be in black and white—a small Italian grocery store impervious to time. In this town of about two thousand, you can enjoy an espresso as you browse some of the world's finest imported Italian oils, vinegars, pestos, giardinieras, olives, pastas, sweets and coffee. You can sample the cheese and sausage, as well as Lovera's private-label dressings, sauces and condiments, like the Lovera's World Famous Old World Style Spaghetti Sauce bearing Madeline's picture.

With the family recipes in play, Sam built the small sausage and cheese factories in 1994, and soon every independent grocer worth its salt started carrying Lovera's sausage and cheeses.

"We'd always made cheese and sausage at the store," Sam said. "But it was always just enough for the store. It was always really good, so I decided to start a mail-order business."

Great idea—but he was in no way prepared for what it would take. He'd grown up eating the homemade caciocavallo commonly crafted in home after home in Pittsburg County.

"We always made our own sausage. We were known for it," Sam said. "But the cheese and bread we bought from local ladies and sold it."

The most popular cheese in Pittsburg County was and is caciocavallo, which in Italy carries as much significance as Parmigiano-Reggiano and Gorgonzola. It bears a distinctive flavor that is salty, sharp and creamy. It's no surprise that neither Mike Lovera nor his mother ever made caciocavallo because it's derived from the cattle-herding culture of southern Italy and is as common to the regions of Calabria, Campania, Molise, Puglia, Basilicata and Sicily as Kraft singles in a suburban supermarket. In Italy, it can be melted with tomatoes in phyllo, shaved over pasta, grilled over a wood fire or cut into wedges and served in lieu of meat as a secondo during a meal.

Like so much of classic Italian cuisine, caciocavallo is the result of peasant ingenuity. It is a "pasta filata," or stretched curd. So, too, are mozzarella and provolone, with which caciocavallo shares similiarities in taste and texture. Sam had sold this stuff all his life, and the people who made it were just simple folks like him, so he was sure it couldn't be too complicated.

He was wrong.

"I had all kinds of trouble in the beginning," he said. "I was doing a raw milk cheese, which is what we always ate growing up, but there was no consistency at all."

And it not being pasteurized was leaving him open to all kinds of trouble.

"It was getting so bad, I was worried I might really be putting the store in jeopardy," Sam said.

In an act of desperation, he enrolled in a cheese-making seminar in North America's foremost purveyor of cheese, Wisconsin.

"I learned so much at that thing," he said with a dismissive laugh. "The guy answered every question I'd ever had going through the process over the years."

Armed with new knowledge, Sam went about making a consistent, delicious caciocavallo that has only improved over time. Today, Sam Lovera likes to say the world is shrinking. He recognized the phenomena in the early 1990s when mail-order catalogs were filling mailboxes around the country. Mail order was the impetus for his taking over the cheese manufacturing. Mail order is what allowed him to stave off elimination by grocery giants after taking over the family business. When the Internet sent mail-order catalogs back into the niche market they came from, Sam again adapted, building a website that draws numerous customers daily from around the world. While he never got to live in Europe, the world ended up coming to Sam Lovera.

In 1996, Mikey and his wife moved away from Krebs, leaving the business in his little brother's hands. Mikey first moved to Plano and now resides in Tampa,

Florida. Mary Lovera, named after her aunt, lived in Holland for eight years before settling in New York City. Sam's aunt Mary continued working for her nephew when she wasn't traveling the world. Mary educated Sam and Mikey when he was still around, with stories of growing up in Krebs and the hardship their family had overcome to establish and sustain themselves in Pittsburg County. Mary Lovera Pliska worked at the store forty years. She retired at the age of eighty, twelve years before her death in 2010. Her legacy is the family operation Lovera's continues to be. Just as Sam and Mikey took the baton from their father, Sam has teamed with a member of his family to solidify the future of Lovera's.

Sam and Domenica's oldest daughter, Rachel, married Shawn Duffy, who has been the primary cheesemonger for Lovera's since 2006. In August 2012, Shawn trekked to Raleigh, North Carolina, for the American Cheese Society's annual national conference and brought back silver in the category of Italian-style cheeses. Finishing first and third was national cheese giant BelGioioso's.

Duffy was born in Pennsylvania but moved to Oklahoma at age eight. Working in restaurants since he was old enough, as well as while he worked toward a degree in ecology, Shawn's scientific background is a perfect fit for cheese-making.

"There's so much you can do with cheese," Shawn said. "Once you learn the process, you start to see the possibilities."

The award-winning Caciocavera they make is a caciocavallo-style cheese.

"We can't call it caciocavallo; it's a 'D.O.P.' thing," Sam said.

The D.O.P.—Denominazione d'Origine Protetta—means "Protection of Designation of Origin." Just like sparkling wine not grown in the Champagne region of France can't be called champagne, provolone-mozzarella-style cheese stretched, brined, dried, hung and aged outside of Italy can't be called Caciocavallo.

"We just combined caciocavallo and Lovera to get Caciocavera."

And that's the name that was on the cheese that finished second at the conference in the category of Italian-style cheeses.

"It was our first year to compete, so it is the only cheese we brought," he said. "Next time, we will bring more."

"It's the first time we ever entered anything like that," Sam said. "The notes we got from the judge were really incredible. One judge wrote it was the most exciting new cheese he'd tasted at the competition."

In December 2012, judges from the United States, Spain, France, Italy, Belgium, Switzerland, Denmark, Germany, Greece, South Africa, Portugal and Russia sent more hardware Duffy's way at the United Kingdom's Guild of Fine Food's World Cheese Awards. The Caciocavera cheese received a gold medal in the mild provolone category. The Hickory Smoked

Caciocavera was awarded silver in the smoked cheese category, and the "Batista," a caciocavallo-style fifty-fifty blend of La Mancha goat's milk and Jersey cow's milk, took silver in the mixed milk category.

Shawn says the secret of Lovera's award-winning cheese is sixty miles southwest down the coal belt, in Coal County's Clarita, which is home to an Amish encampment and farmer John Miller.

"Those guys do everything right," Duffy said. "I've never been down there, any time of year, when the cows aren't grazing on the most amazing green pastures, and they rotate them to protect the land. The milk I get from them is so filled with butter-fat it's almost completely yellow."

Nothing determines the integrity of artisan cheese like the quality of the milk, Shawn says.

Huddled around a bin of steaming water, Shawn, Sam and two or three others draw balls of fermented curd and warm whey that they stretch, work and manipulate into gourd shapes. From there, the gourds are submerged in cold water to set. Then the gourds go into a bin full of brine. The salt penetrates the cheese, which helps reduce the risk of bad bacteria and adds flavor. Finally, they are hung from the ceiling. In Italy, the gourds were tied on each end of a rope, with one end slung over high beam and left to hang on either side like saddlebags, which is where the name caciocavallo is derived, meaning "cheese on horseback."

In May 2013, Lovera's finished installation of a drying room that will allow it to increase its production as well as its offerings.

"I'm in this business 'cause when I grew up, we lived upstairs over the store, and it was just what we did," Sam said. "In a business like this, you've got to have kids willing to carry on the tradition. Shawn here will probably be the one."

Family has always been the glue that binds Lovera's, but it's the fresh Caciocavera hanging over the back counter also filled with steaks, chops, chicken, pancetta, prosciutto, capicola, salami, bologna, mortadella and, of course, house-made sausage that keeps people coming back.

If you sit for very long on one of the benches on the porch, you're bound to shake hands with a lot of strangers and say hello to locals while sipping an espresso while you decide which sausage you're going to take home and how big a gourd of cheese you want to buy. If the weather is right and the birds are singing, it's very difficult not to think about heaven. And if heaven is a place drawn from your heart, then meat-and-cheese lovers who say their prayers and do unto others as they'd have done unto them will doubtlessly find habitation in the hereafter where all the gold-paved roads lead to Lovera's and a cold bottle of Choc on the porch.

Chapter 12

KREBS UNBOUND

One of the miracles of the Pittsburg County culinary history is how conservative it's been over the years. In the eight decades since the first prairie Italian restaurant opened, it's hard to believe it wasn't until the 1990s that any of the families started trying to generate interest in their products beyond the borders of coal country. But it's easy to understand when you have that many people coming to you every week.

Today, Lovera's is starting to make its mark with its artisan cheese and sausage, as is Pete's Place with Choc beer. In the early 2000s, Dom Giacomo's great-niece Vicki Muhs moved to South Padre Island with no intention of opening a restaurant.

Her mother, Rose Ann Robertson, said, "Pretty soon Vicki called me up and said, 'Oh, mama, I miss the restaurant business,' so I told her, 'Let's open one up down there.'" Not long after, Gabriella's was born on South Padre Island.

Muhs has always loved to cook, dating back to her Isle of Capri upbringing. Her family's restaurants might be entrenched in telling the story of the past, but Vicki is intent on exploring the possibilities of the future. Vicki, whose daughter Stephanie Fields, helps run the Isle of Capri today, grew up waiting tables at the family restaurant and learning to cook her family recipes. Within the enormous confines of the Isle of Capri kitchen is a breakfast table where some locals come to sit, sip, gab and nosh. It was also a training ground for young Vicki, who has a passion for cooking as bright as the neon sign out front.

Pete Prichard in his signature chef's hat at Pete's Place. *Courtesy of the Prichard family.*

"I wanted to share the food I grew up with, and the best food we made was at home," Vicki said. "After a few years, my husband could tell I missed cooking so he asked me if I wanted to open a restaurant, and I said 'Yes.' So, we got everything together and opened Gabriella's on South Padre Island."

Rose Ann said they started in one spot in Port Isabel, Texas, just across the bridge from South Padre, but it wasn't a great location.

"Once we got the spot on the island, where everything is, things just took off." The restaurant succeeded for ten years before the chance to return to the red dirt of Oklahoma finally presented itself.

"We had a great time down in Texas, but we always wanted to come home," Vicki said. So they did, but rather than home to Krebs, the Muhs opted to open in Oklahoma City, taking over a building with even more history than either the Isle of Capri. Gabriella's is not only rooted in Oklahoma history by blood but also by bricks and mortar. It resides in the space last occupied by the County Line Barbecue, but most notoriously by the Kentucky Club, which was known for gambling, shady ladies and

Vicki Muhs is the first to take the flavors of Pittsburg County outside of southeast Oklahoma with Gabriella's in South Padre Island, Texas, and Oklahoma City. *Photo used with permission from the* Oklahoman.

scandalous busts. The building first housed the Silver Club in 1935, followed by the Oakcliff Nite Club and then the Kentucky Club in 1938. The building survived raids, a major fire and Father Time, though in recent years it had begun to show its age. But having an experienced contractor in the family paid serious dividends.

"My husband did a great job on this place," Vicki said. "The place was in pretty bad shape."

Once through the door, it's immediately apparent the place has been overhauled. A new deli counter is a few paces south of the entry, decorated with faux grapevines. The County Line, an upscale barbecue concept born in Austin, Texas, had embraced 1940s culture and installed private rooms around the perimeter of the restaurant, giving it a bit of a Pete's Place feel.

The place still has enough creaks to remind you that you're walking through a historic building. The south end of the restaurant includes a bar, large windows overlooking the city and an open kitchen where you'll see both Vicki and her daughter Ashton Gabriella, for whom the restaurant is named, toiling over the stove or next to the wood-fired oven built in Italy.

"Uncle Dom was insistent that we have an open kitchen," Rose Ann said. "So I told Vicki, 'You've got to have an open kitchen.'" Diners can even watch the ballet of sauté pans, pizza cutters and pasta slinging from a kitchen-side seat.

Like the Isle of Capri and GiaComo's before it, Gabriella's is the sum of the family's efforts. Aside from Vicki and Ashton in the kitchen and Duane tending the building, son Mike makes all the sausage from his own recipe and is pitmaster of the smoker left behind by the County Line, while his brother Brandon works on the business and marketing side.

The one derivation Vicki has made from her great-uncle Dom's recipe for success is the menu. While the Isle has expanded its menu some since the early days, Gabriella's has a four-page dinner menu that includes all the pastas, pizza, steaks, chicken and lamb fries you expect, but it also includes lots of seafood, which Vicki grew a kinship for during her time in South Padre Island. The Coal Miner's Spaghetti is a tribute to her upbringing, but it's a carbonara topped with an egg rather than anything you'd find in Krebs. The Pistacchi Linguine is not to be missed. It is a creamy mix of shallots, peas and garlic with toasted and ground pistachios in a parmesan-cream sauce that binds to the pasta in holy matrimony. Want something to drink? They've got plenty selections from the Krebs Brewing Company. They also carry Lovera's cheese and some homemade sausage.

Aside from a new aging room, the Loveras recently took control of a cheese factory in Ada, Oklahoma, where Shawn believes he will be able to expand the Lovera's repertoire to include sheep's milk gorgonzola and other variations on Italian classics.

Meanwhile, the Krebs Brewing Company, under Zachary Prichard's watch, is spreading its brand all the way back to the land where Luca Piegari left for Pittsburg County with no end in sight. His two sisters, Katie and Blair, also share a passion for the business. Katie is training to become the general manager, while Blair has an eye toward the oven.

While the culinary traditions of Pittsburg County have always done just fine within its own confines, this forward thinking among the principal families can't do anything but fortify them. After all, forward

The Pete's Place family, from left: Josh and Katie Walters, Kathy, Joe, Blair and Zachary Prichard. *Courtesy of the Prichard family.*

thinking is what established the traditions in the first place. This kind of action taken without having to stare down starvation bodes well for the future of Pittsburg County cuisine. Some will say the growth is a long time in coming. But those folks don't understand the recipe for success was born of desperation and cultivated by conservative growth. Part of the magic of Pittsburg County fare is its imperviousness to time. It's as if the community subconsciously feared any step outside the county line would expose their precious ravioli, lamb fries and Choc to a vampire's fate in the face of sunshine.

Regardless of the reasons for conservatism, it's worked. People still crowd into the four restaurants and Lovera's Italian Market every weekend in hordes. They don't come to be transported to an Italian villa; they come for a slice of history, a heaping helping of tradition and to be reassured that some good things really do last. What they get besides good food in Pittsburg County is living, thriving proof of how working together bolsters community.

"I like to think we work as a whole here," Joe Prichard said in one of our first interviews for this book. "I'm not sure any of us would survive if even one of us failed."

Family meal before service at Pete's Place. *Courtesy of the Prichard family.*

So they cook on in Pittsburg County. And even though you can get on the Internet and reel in sauces, sausage, cheese and even Choc, there is no substitute for a visit to the coal-rich hills of southeastern Oklahoma for a taste of the frontier time from which it still slowly thaws.

CHOCTAW CUISINE

When coal mining began in the Choctaw Nation, there was initial upheaval among the tribe. However, when the United States federal government offered the tribe a stake in the profits, the furor died down. The Choctaw people were no stranger to being abused during the European colonization of their home. Starting in 1830, the Choctaws were forced from their ancestral homes in the Deep South and directed to the new Choctaw Nation in Oklahoma after the Civil War, which was less than twenty years before coal mining began in earnest along the coal belt. For millennia before that, Choctaw cooks developed traditional foods like *tanchi labona*, *pvlvska bvnaha*, (banana bread), and *walakshi* (fruit dumplings).

But the native peoples were practicing local and sustainable food practices before anyone speaking English could set foot on North American soil, much less makeup a word like "locavore." So when the tribe was moved, much of the traditional food was lost as it had all been based on local ingredients. Pittsburg County is a lush land, but when the Choctaws arrived, the hills were being ravaged by railroad construction and coal mining. Their nation contained greener pastures outside present-day Pittsburg County, and they settled more abundantly away from the coal mines. Nevertheless, the culinary traditions of the Choctaw people survive today and are well preserved by their government.

For this book, I made a request to the Choctaw Nation to include some of their culinary traditions. With permission from the Choctaw Nation, here is a description of the native cuisine and traditions of some of this country's oldest inhabitants.

Nipi Shila, (a Choctaw term that used to refer to "jerky") must be one of the oldest ancestral Choctaw foods. The earliest recipe for Nipi Shila was simply to cut lean meat into thin, narrow strips and suspend them over a smoky fire. This preserved the meat by drying it and exposing it to creosote in the smoke.

Today, this technique can be seen firsthand in deer jerky–making demonstrations at the Choctaw Labor Day Festival. The same basic technique was surely used by their ancestors fourteen thousand years ago on the meat from now-extinct animals. Similar drying methods have also been used by Choctaws for thousands of years to preserve fish and fruit.

In the spring, women collected leaves from young, succulent plants such as poke, dock and stinging nettles, providing the Vitamin A, calcium and iron needed to supplement dried food rations that had been stored over the winter. In the summer, they collected edible fruits, like grapes and blackberries; grains, like sumpweed seeds; and oily hickory nuts, while the men provided protein by fishing and hunting small game. In the fall, women gathered acorns, while the men hunted the larger animals that the acorns attracted. Hunter's quarry provided meat and hides to protect the tribes during winter. In the winter, the community dug starchy tubers like greenbrier roots and welcomed the Vitamin C provided by fresh persimmons.

Before the birth of pottery, the Choctaw cooked in the coals of fires, steamed foods in leaves, roasted or smoked foods on racks over open flame, boiled foods in containers made of animal hides and buried foods in the earth and baked them. Some of the foods prepared in ancient times are still eaten by Choctaw people today.

Europeans came to Choctaw country in waves, beginning with the Spanish, then French, English and finally Americans. Each of these groups borrowed and shared foods with the Choctaws and other Southeastern tribes, creating new blends and cooking styles.

When the Spanish arrived in Choctaw country in the mid 1500s, they brought *shukha* (pigs), *wak* (cattle), *takkon* (peaches) and *shukshi*, (watermelons), which the Choctaw quickly incorporated into the diet. Traditional Choctaw foods such as *Shukha Nipi* (pork roast) and *Nipi Shila* (salted pork) or any of the many traditional dishes that include pork roast, bacon, ham, beef, peaches or watermelon exist because of early interactions with the Spanish.

In return, the Choctaws and other Southeastern and Mesoamerican tribes gave the Spanish the corn and bean varieties that native farmers had been selectively crossing and developing for generations. These were eventually given to the rest of the world. Today, corn is the third-most important food crop worldwide.

In the early 1700s, when the French, with their African slaves, began establishing permanent settlements in the Choctaw homeland, the sharing and blending of ethnic foods led to the creation of a whole new style of cuisine, known today as Cajun food. In the creation of Cajun cuisine, the French contributed their traditional stews and wheat flour. The Spanish contributed onions, garlic, tomatoes and peppers. African cooks contributed okra and field peas. Choctaws contributed several essential elements, including an intimate knowledge of local fish, shellfish and native plant and animal foods. Choctaw people gathered sassafras leaves and sold or traded them in towns to produce filé, a traditional Choctaw stew thickener, and a vital ingredient in Cajun gumbo.

Written records from this time period indicate that the Choctaw were the most productive agricultural producers in the Southeast. By the mid-1700s, Choctaw farmers had developed knowledge of European vegetables and were growing crops of leeks, garlic, cabbage and other non-native plants for the purpose of exporting them to the French colonies for their food.

With contact with the United States in the late 1700s and the passage of more than two centuries have come many changes in the diets of most Choctaw people. These changes have been brought about as a result of relocation through the Trail of Tears, boarding schools, commodity rations, changes in cooking technology and a shift to highly processed foods. Native crops have also been altered. Hybrid and genetically modified seed varieties, easy to grow through mechanized agriculture but often relatively low in nutrition, have been selected in place of the older, more nutritious native seed varieties. Ironically, today some "traditional" Choctaw meals, such as Indian tacos, include not a single ingredient that was in Choctaw diets four hundred years ago—not even the type of corn used to make the vegetable oil.

The loss is tragic, but thanks to a dedication to preserving Choctaw heritage by the few, there is hope that traditional techniques might rise again as they have in so many styles of cuisine. Many other very old traditional Choctaw corn and bean dishes were made in the past and continue to be favorite foods today: *Tanchi Lakchi*, or corn grits; *Ampi Hobi*, corn on the cob; *Tanchi Vlwasha*, fried corn; *Tanchi Apusha*, roasted corn; *Pvlvska*, cornbread; *Pvlvska Mihlofa*, "grated bread"; *Pvlvska Hawuksho*, "sour bread"; *Poskalvwsha*, "hot water bread"; *Pvlvska Holbi*, "bread in the shucks"; *Bvla Okchi*, bean porridge; and *Bvla Hobbi*, boiled beans.

Europeans came to Choctaw country in waves, beginning with the Spanish, then French, English and finally Americans. Each of these groups borrowed and shared foods with the Choctaws and other Southeastern tribes, creating new blends and cooking styles.

The Choctaw were among the most productive agricultural producers in the Southeast. By the mid-1700s, Choctaw farmers had developed knowledge of European vegetables and were growing crops of leeks, garlic, cabbage and other non-native plants for the purpose of exporting them to the French colonies. As a result of relocation through the Trail of Tears, boarding schools, commodity rations, changes in cooking technology and a shift to highly processed foods the Choctaw diet was adversely affected. Native crops have also been altered. Hybrid and genetically modified seed varieties, easy to grow through mechanized agriculture but often relatively low in nutrition, have been selected in place of the older, more nutritious native seed varieties. Ironically, today some "traditional" Choctaw meals, such as Indian tacos, include not a single ingredient that was in Choctaw diets four hundred years ago—not even the type of corn used to make the vegetable oil.

The following are summaries of early written recipes for traditional Choctaw foods, which, based on their ingredients and cooking techniques, have probably been made for thousands of years:

Koshiba, or poke salad: Pick small poke leaves in the spring, when they are tender and before they become bitter. Put young leaves in water, and boil for a short time. Pour off water and boil again, with fat meat if desired. The same process may also be followed to prepare dock and stinging nettles. Leaves from the lamb's-quarter plant do not require parboiling and can be eaten all summer.

Uksak Ulhkomo, or hickory nut oil: This broth is traditionally added to many Choctaw dishes. Hickory nuts have very hard shells. To make *Uksak Ulhkomo*, hickory nuts can be crushed and placed in a cloth sack that is boiled in stew and then removed, leaving behind the "hickory milk." This technique avoids the work of picking the meat from the shells.

Uksak Alhanta, or mixed hickory nuts: Crack open and pick out meat. Discard shells. Pound meat into a paste. Put paste in boiling water and stir briskly. Serve as a porridge.

Nusi Pvlvska, or acorn bread: Hull live oak acorns and pound them into flour. Place acorn flour in a cane sieve near a creek. Dip water over the acorns until the bitterness leaves. Mix the acorn flour with water to make a thick paste. Wrap paste around a stick and hold over a fire until done. Similar bread can also be made from beechnuts, hazelnuts and chinquapins. In times of scarcity, bread was sometimes made from flour created from boiled pine roots.

Okshush, or acorn pudding: is made by mixing acorn flour with water and boiling to make a mush.

Ukof Honni, or persimmon stew: Gather persimmons in winter after a frost. If they are gathered too soon, they will be full of tannic acid and inedible. Some trees produce very sweet fruit, while others can have a bitter taste. To prepare, remove the skins and seeds from the fruit. Leave as chunks or mash into a pulp. Cut meat into bite-sized pieces and throw into boiling water. Add persimmon pulp or chunks. The stew may be thickened with hickory nut oil or acorn flour.

Ahelusa, or "black potato": Made from the roots of the trailing wildbean (*Strophostyles helvola*), these are dug up, cleaned, boiled in water and then mashed.

Lukckuk Ahe, or "mud potato": The white-fleshed roots from the groundnut (*Apios americana*) are dug up, collected and washed. They are then boiled in water and served as "Irish potatoes" are today. Alternatively, mud potatoes were sometimes cooked in the coals of a fire.

Kantak Pvlvska, or "greenbrier root bread": This is made from the roots of a thorny vine, common in the Southeastern woods. The roots are dug up, collected and washed. The outside of the root is then peeled off. While still in a moist state, the inner portions of the roots are pounded in a mortar to form a paste. The paste is made into cakes, which are fried in bear's oil. Alternatively, the roots can be dried before pounding and made into flour.

Many traditional Choctaw dishes incorporate corn and beans as ingredients. Some of these, such as *Oksak Bahpo* (a mush made from pounded hickory nuts, walnuts and corn), combined older Choctaw foods with the new crops. Other dishes were made solely from the new foods. Based on their ingredients, the following Choctaw corn recipes likely date back before European contact but are probably no older than one thousand years:

Pvlvska Bvnaha, or banana bread: Cornmeal is mixed with pea hull ash and water to form dough. To this, cooked beans may be added, if desired. The dough is formed into masses, wrapped into green corn husks and tied. These are then boiled. A related dish, *Oksak Atahap*, can be made in the same manner, except with the addition of hickory nutmeat instead of peas or beans.

Tafula, or hominy (literally, boiled corn): Boil corn kernels in a large pot. Lye (wood ash) is added and the boiling continued until the cornhusks begin to loosen. Afterward, the corn is washed in clean water and beaten in a mortar to remove its husks and break up the kernels. These cleaned kernels can be dried or put back in water and cooked until soft. Sour hominy, *Tafula Hawushko*, is made by keeping cooked hominy in a warm place until it has soured. Alternatively to the souring process, beans and/or hickory nut oil may be added to the hominy. If beans are added, the dish may be called *Tafula Toni Ibulhtoh*.

Tanchi Labona (literally, stirred corn): The Tafula-making process is followed as described above, except instead of removing the corn husks in a mortar, they are taken off by rubbing in the hands. This leaves the kernels whole. To make *Tanchi Labona*, meat is added to the hominy, which is then boiled in a deep pot. Today, this meat is normally pork roast. This dish is often called *Pashofa*, its Chickasaw name.

Tanchi Okchi, or sagamité: This stew happens to be the first known written Choctaw recipe, dating back to 1755. To make it, dried corn kernels are removed from the ears and ground in a mortar. The best of the results are collected and saved. The coarser meal is stirred into boiling water. Pumpkin and/or beans and bean leaves are added to the stew. When nearly done, the broth is thickened with the fine corn meal that was saved after grinding. The stew can be flavored with lye made from corn silk or bean pods.

Bota Kapvssa, or cold cornmeal: This was the food of Choctaw warriors in the field. It was made by boiling corn kernels in a pot over a fire until they begin to swell. Remove and partially dry. Place back into a dry, heated pot and stir continually until they become a parched brown color. Beat in a mortar and then sift in a fanner basket to remove the hulls. Return to mortar and beat until a fine meal is obtained. For consumption, the meal is mixed with water and allowed to sit, forming a thick, soup-like beverage.

Walakshi, or fruit dumplings: Served as a sweet dish, *Walakshi* are a traditional Choctaw food for weddings. The oldest recipes include dumplings made from cornmeal. These were boiled in water with native fruits like grapes or blackberries.

Appendix II
CONTEMPORARY RECIPES

Pete Prichard rests after a hard night in the kitchen at Pete's Place. *Courtesy of the Prichard family.*

Krebs Sausage

Sam Lovera said his sausage is a northern Italian recipe, which doesn't include fennel. However, Lovera's now offers a variety of sausages. Here's a basic recipe with a couple optional variations.

INGREDIENTS
3- to 5-pound pork shoulder
½ cup chopped fresh garlic
⅓ cup ground paprika
¼ cup salt
2 tablespoons fresh ground black pepper

OPTIONAL INGREDIENTS
1 tablespoon red pepper flakes
1 tablespoon fennel

DIRECTIONS
Grind the pork through a meat grinder into a large bowl. Combine with remaining ingredients thoroughly, and let stand over night. Run through mixture again, and stuff directly into hog casing.
Source: Sam Lovera

Polenta with Lovera's Italian Sausage

One item you won't find at Pete's Place, Roseanna's, the Isle of Capri and GiaComo's is polenta, because it's a northern Italian staple. But the Loveras came from the north, so it's a favorite in the Lovera household. Sammy likes the simple stuff, and it doesn't get any simpler than polenta.

"It's just cornmeal," Sammy laughs when the subject comes up. "But it's great, and I love it."

Polenta was and is an alternative to pasta, which has become more popular in the United States in the past decade.

INGREDIENTS
4 cups water
1½ teaspoons salt
1½ cups yellow corn meal
1 pound Lovera's Italian sausage cut from casing
5 cups Lovera's Famous Old World Spaghetti Sauce
½ cup grated Parmesan cheese

DIRECTIONS

Bring water to a boil in a large pot. When water is in a full boil, add salt. Gradually add corn meal, stirring constantly to keep from scorching. Reduce heat to low and cook uncovered 30 minutes, stirring frequently until mixture is thick and smooth. Spread in ungreased square baking dish. Cover and keep warm.

Heat a skillet over medium heat and brown sausage in it. Once browned, strain off grease, return to skillet over medium-low heat and stir in sauce. Simmer over medium-low to low heat 15 to 20 minutes.

By now, the polenta will have set in the baking dish. Slice polenta into squares and serve topped with sausage mixture and top with Parmesan cheese.

Source: Sam Lovera

Choctaw Beer

Longtime Pittsburg County resident Marion Fassino says he doesn't use a recipe to make Choc beer, nor did anyone who taught him. He says he learned strictly by observation. Here is a recipe from another Pittsburg County lifer, Michael Lalli, who knows a little bit about brewing.

You'll need a ten-gallon bucket or crock, a muslin bag or lots of cheesecloth, sterilized bottles, a bottle-capper and rubber-tubing to siphon the finished Choc out of the crock and into the bottles.

INGREDIENTS
2 ounces liberty hop pellets
6 pounds 2-row barley malt
10 gallons water
5 pounds cane sugar
2 packages EDME ale yeast

DIRECTIONS

Place the barley malt and hops in a muslin bag or wrap it them in cheesecloth and bind the top. Pillow cases are traditionally used but aren't optimal.

Add to pot of ten gallons of water. Bring the temperature of the water up to 150 degrees and hold for one hour. Remove the grain and top water level back up to ten gallons and add sugar.

When the temperature of the finished beer has cooled to 70 degrees or below, add the yeast. Ferment at 65 to 70 degrees until the yeast has stopped working—Marion says three days, but Michael says it can be up to fourteen.

To bottle, dissolve one cup of sugar in one quart of boiling water, after it has cooled add to beer and bottle. Store at room temperature for seven to ten days.

Chill, pop the top and look for blue smoke.

Shetone (Italian Easter Quiche)

In Liguria, this dish is served only during Holy Week and is called Torta Pasqualina. This recipe was shared by Joe Prichard. The spelling of Shetone is a complete guess on his part. Every Catholic in the area, and especially those of any Italian descent, call it Shetone or Zhetone. Joe's best guess is that it's a slang term, and since his Italian isn't too good and mine nonexistent, we're not going to venture any guesses. It is, however, worth noting that the original Ligurian recipe does share the name of Pete Prichard's first wife, Pasqualina. Something to chew on while you're putting this one together right before Easter. Joe's recipe is big, as he makes enough to take to church and have enough to serve friends at an impromptu bull session at the Krebs Brewing Co. warehouse.

FOR THE CRUST (THIS COVERS TWO 9-BY-12 CASSEROLE DISHES, ABOUT 24 SERVINGS)

6 cups all-purpose flour

1½ teaspoons salt

1 tablespoon sugar

½ teaspoon baking powder

2 eggs beaten

1 cup plus 2 tablespoons shortening

1½ cups water

FOR THE FILLING

42 eggs

3 pounds cured ham, cubed

1 pound muenster cheese, grated

1 pound Longhorn cheese, grated

DIRECTIONS

Preheat oven to 350 degrees.

Sift flour, salt, baking powder and sugar. Combine all the crust ingredients in a large mixing bowl, reserving the two additional tablespoons of shortening, and carefully knead into dough.

Grease casseroles with shortening and press the crusts into the casseroles. Bake for 15 minutes, then remove and let cool to avoid cooking the eggs on contact.

In a large mixing bowl, beat the eggs for the filling. Thoroughly mix in remaining ingredients.

Pour filling over raw crusts, and bake until eggs crusts have turned golden brown, about 1 hour and 25 minutes.

Source: Joe Prichard

Lamb Fries

Where to begin with this recipe…First, the good news: it's as simple a recipe as you'll find. Now the bad: finding lamb testicles in a retail market will be a challenge. Once you overcome that hurdle, you will have to remove the protective membrane. If at all possible, have that done by a butcher. Even still, you will hold these bits in your hand and sink a knife into them. I daresay this will be one dirty job women might be able to do, at least the first time—especially if they are angry at any males in their life.

Now that we've got that part squared away, here's a recipe from Joe Prichard of Pete's Place.

INGREDIENTS
lamb or calf testicles
cracker meal, finely ground
salt
pepper

DIRECTIONS

Let the testicles soak in water about fifteen minutes. Pat dry, slice to desired thickness and dredge in cracker meal with salt and pepper to taste. Deep-fry in 350-degree oil until golden brown. Serve with fresh lemon and cocktail sauce.

Source: Joe Prichard

Italian Salad with Lombarda Sauce

Finding Italian recipes was impossible before World War I, thanks to the less-than-erudite gatekeepers of the American household at Good Housekeeping and their contemporaries. I was able to find this Italian recipe in one of Krebs' five newspapers that existed during the coal boom. This recipe ran exactly as follows in the Oklahoma Miner of February 26, 1920, under the heading, "The Kitchen Cabinet."

ITALIAN SALAD: Cut one carrot and one turnip into slices, and let cook in boiling broth or soup. When cold, add two cold, boiled potatoes and one beet, cut into strips. Add a tablespoon of chopped leeks or scarped onion pulp and mix. Pour over the following sauce and garnish with watercress.

LOMBARDA SAUCE: Cook one-fourth cupful of flour in one-fourth cupful of hot butter; add half a teaspoonful of salt, one-fourth teaspoonful of paprika, and one cupful of jellied chicken broth (I teaspoon of chicken base will probably do the trick); stir until boiling hot. Set over boiling water, and beat one-fourth of a cupful of butter, beaten to a cream with two egg yolks and the juice of half a lemon. As soon as the egg is cooked, beat in three fourths of a cupful of thick tomato sauce. When cold and ready to use, add one teaspoonful of parsley, chopped very fine.

The recipe above was the first one in a group about seasonal dishes preceded by the following quote by Ralph Waldo Emerson that seems appropriate as we reach the end of this tome:

Finish every day and be done with it. You have done what you could, some blunders and absurdities no doubt crept in; forget them as soon as you can. Tomorrow is a new day; you shall begin it well and serenely and with too high a spirit to be cumbered with your old nonsense.

INDEX

ABOUT THE AUTHOR

Dave Cathey is the food editor of the *Oklahoman* in Oklahoma City, the author of "The Food Dude" column and host of *Open Flame*, a newsok. com program spotlighting local restaurants and cooking demonstrations. Dave holds a bachelor's in journalism from Oklahoma Christian University and a master's in creative writing from the University of Central Oklahoma. His work has appeared in *Saveur* and *Food Network* magazine. He lives in Oklahoma City with his wife, Lori; son, Luke; and daughter, Kate.